Sir Prize the Storm Pony

Braving the Storms of Life

Written By:
Carin Thamke

Contributions By:
Missy Neale

Eli,
Thank you for coming
tonight! It was so
amazing to meet
you. Carin
Thamke

ACKNOWLEDGEMENTS

This book has been three years in the making, the idea and inspiration started in the spring of 2019. The time I spent with Sir Prize has a huge place in my heart for so many reasons. But the journey of writing this book was just as humbling and just as rewarding.

I want to acknowledge several people for supporting my journey:

to my husband, Pete – you dedicate your heart and kindness to everyone; and you are so loved by many because of it. You are my person. I am truly blessed to call you husband.

to our children – watching you grow into individual spirits with different tastes and ambitions have been amazing to watch; we cannot wait to see how your future unfolds. We love you dearly!

to my parents – you dedicate your life to caring for others and the land. You have built the foundations of who I am. My love for agriculture and nature are ever living because of you.

to my friend, Missy – you dedicate your life to caring for animals, teaching others to understand them and respect them. My time with you and Sir Prize were some of the happiest moments in my life. Thank you for your friendship and for the feeling of "home away from home".

to my pre-readers – Madelyn E., Rebeka (Beka) N., Amya A., Toddi S., Grechen Biller, and the 2021-2022 6th grade class at Jefferson Intermediate and Ms Christen Dannenbrink, – you committed time out of your day to pre-read this story. Without your review and feedback, this book would not be what it is today. Thank you!

CONTENTS

PREFACE

This book is based on the real-life events of the pony, Sir Prize. The locations of the stories are in the suburbs of Los Angeles, CA (1980s and 1990s) and suburbs of Town and Country, MO (early 2000s) The events and stories are based on Carin's and Missy's memories, but they are spun into Sir Prize's point of view. There are pictures throughout the book to provide the reader with true-event contexts. They were taken between 1980s to 2004, the days before common, digital photography. Many of the conversations that are listed may be paraphrased to maintain the storyline; however, each major event from his name to the moves are all true.

There are lessons to be learned from the journeys of Sir Prize. We must:

- learn to be patient when working with animals
- use positive re-enforcement with animals where possible
- be aware and sensitive if a situation may cause an animal discomfort or nervousness
- be mindful of your surroundings if you live in a suburb or city that has large animals that may move from place to place; give them space
- above all, be respectful of any animal and its tendencies. Example, if a horse is scared, it may kick with its back legs. (And that, my friends, hurt!)

I wrote this in honor of Sir Prize and what his voice may have been as he experienced exciting and scary moments throughout "storms" or "calms" of his life. We hope that by reading this book you will spread kindness to others just as others have shared their kindness with us.

A SURPRISE DELIVERY

The newborn colt opened his eyes to the dark world around him, all his senses were in overdrive. The smells, the sights, the sounds - all of it was overwhelming. He lied there on the ground, just taking it all in. The light breeze moved his silky, black fur in soothing waves. He felt his mother licking his back, grunting a few times, and nudging him to get up. Not yet knowing night from day, the colt just assumed the darkness around him was normal. His eyes adjusted more to his surroundings, instincts knocking at his nerves. The area had odd shadows with a single bright light in the distance. The shadows shaped into a corral fence right next to him and a nearby barn or small shelter. The smell of his mother's musty breath calmed his breathing. The night was still, as if the stars themselves anxiously held their twinkles for this little one's first stand.

Waves of awareness provided motivation for his first wobbly movements. The colt adjusted his legs underneath him, concentrating, *Is this how I do it?* His mother continued to grunt, nudging harder now. *Alright, alright! Give me a minute, Mom!*

He adjusted his weight forward to shift his back legs out, lifting his rump a little higher. He leaned forward to lift off his front hooves. *Ouch!* His head stopped abruptly on the bottom rung of the corral fence. It knocked him down to the ground. He wiggled his legs awkwardly, concentration intensified. *This standing thing is hard,* he thought. He stuck his rear in the air, which put his nose directly in the dirt. *Ugh* he moaned. He yanked his rump back down to the ground.

Ok, so my head is blocked but my rear is free, he thought to himself. Although scooting back seemed like a logical solution, he was intent on moving forward. He reached his front hooves out, pulling himself forward. He pushed on his back legs again, but this time the same bar bumped his tailbone. *Fine.* He stretched his front hooves again, inching forward slowly and methodically. He uncurled his back legs slowly to push up again, anticipating the bar to stop his progress. *Ok, that worked.* He pushed himself up on his front hooves. He stood there shaking on all fours. *Success! Look Ma!*

Suddenly, a new noise shattered the peaceful night. *What is that?* The colt twitched his ears forward to the piercing and edgy sound. He looked ahead toward the distant light and saw a figure also on all fours but with aggressive jabs at the dark – a dog! Each jab brought that edgy bark; it increased as the dog inched closer to the corral fence. *Oh goodness! It's coming this way!* the colt shook in fear. He leaned harder on the fence, trying to get to his mother. His mother didn't seem to mind the noise as she continued to lick his mane through the corral bars. As another light brightened the night, a voice yelled out for the dog. The dog hesitated, not sure whether to go back as commanded or to go after this unfamiliar stranger. After some strict coaxing, the dog surrendered to the fierce authority.

The slam of the screen door simultaneously eliminated the additional light, snapping the night's hush back into place. It was as if all the plants, animals, and stars themselves held their breath in anticipation of another interruption. The colt franticly moved his eyes around, widening lashes, twitching his ears. *What else?* His heart raced from the sudden disturbance. The sounds of the breeze through the trees slowly magnified, triggering insects to join in the symphony. The colt's ragged breathing returned to normal. *Mom, this place is scary!*

He tried to move closer to his mother, but the fence was still in the way. He strolled a few feet and tried again, the fence forcefully stopping his intentions. *I can't get to you!* he panicked. He continued multiple times to walk a few feet, push toward her, but the cool bars stopped him every time. *Mom? What do I do?* She calmly grunted at him, nuzzling him with her nose through the slots between the bars. Every time he moved, she walked with him, never leaving his side. *I'm right here, son.*

After some time, curiosity and frustration got the best of him. As he explored the fence line, he noticed more shapes in the dark — landscaping with flowers heavily draped over the edges, a water spicket, a tire leaned against a pole. Completely curious in his adventures, he didn't remember the dog and had no perception of potential dangers. Exhaustion consumed him like a fog, legs shaking from the new exercise he completed. *I'll just lie here for a bit,* eyelids heavy as a weighted blanket. He closed his eyes, lashes long and soft on the edge of his face. His body surrendered to sleep. The stars finally twinkled in the night sky, happy with the new addition to the world beneath them.

*****

As hours crept by, the night's darkness yielded to the morning light. The neighborhood started to wake with people picking up their papers, leaving for work, or walking their dogs. All the new noises broke the colt's slumber. He squinted his eyes open, noticing the new brightness around him. The dark shadows and star-sprinkled canopy disappeared. The colt's curiosity spiked as life around him was full of new discoveries. Unfortunately, he was a little weaker than the previous night, stomach rumbled with emptiness. He swayed his head to look back at his mother; she hadn't moved from the spot he last saw her.

Abruptly, a jogger on his morning run stopped in front of him. "Well, hello there, little guy," he said. The jogger slowly approached the colt, hands out to grab the small animal. The colt jerked his head back around in shock, suddenly surprised by this new creature in front of him. He tried to stand up but with no luck. "Shh…it's ok, little guy," said the jogger, as he carefully folded the colt into his arms. "Let's get you home," he continued. *But my mom is right there!* the colt shouted in his mind.

As the jogger consoled the colt, he approached the front of a house where the dog lived. *Oh no – don't take me here!* the colt shuffled in protest. The jogger clumsily reached for the doorbell as he tried to balance the colt in his arms. *Please don't drop me. Please just take me back to my mother.* Abruptly, a dog barked behind the front door. *That's the same bark as last night!* the colt recalled, eyes once again widening in fear. He wiggled in anticipation, making the jogger shift his weight to hold onto him.

Finally, the door opened, and a woman stood at the door. She looked at the jogger, looked at the colt, then looked back at the jogger. "Hello!" she greeted. Her eyes focused to the colt. "What is this?" she asked.

"Um, well, I found him resting right over there," he said as he jerked his head to the side. "You're the only one in this LA suburb that has a horse, so I figured it was yours."

"But, we don't have a baby…" her voice trailed off. The look on her face changed as if she remembered the previous night…dog barking…movement in the corral. Her eyes darted to the dog with his brown fur on guard and stiff, then to the jogger, then finally to the colt in his arms.

"Well, what a surprise you are! Your momma must have been pregnant when we bought her and we didn't even know," she said, placing her hand on her forehead in confusion. She regained composure and gently took the colt from the jogger. The woman's face changed to amusement. "That is your name. 'Surprise'!"

"Surprise" is now my name? the colt pondered. The woman struggled to get her shoes on while holding him, then there was the dog barking and sniffing his legs. Surprise was agitated by all the newness and movement – and very hungry. "Well – meet your little brother!" she

said to the dog, who switched back and forth from barking to sniffing the new animal in his domain. The bark seemed more excited than aggressive now, tail wagging in welcome delight. She shuffled out the back door, the same door the dog entered the previous night, letting the door slam behind her. "Don't worry mama – I got your little one right here!" she cried out to the mare in the corral. Surprise's mother swished her tail anxiously, nodding her head and pacing the fence. Her grunting noises were more enunciated than last night.

"You must be starving if you've been away from her all night," the woman commented as she opened the corral gate. She gently lowered Surprise to the dirt floor. *Oh, thank God*, Surprise sighed. The woman watched as Surprise was finally able to reunite with his mother, throwing her hands on her hips. The dog continued to bark excitedly. "Calm down," she laughed "and play nice!"

*****

Days passed and Surprise got used to his surroundings. He never really learned the woman's name, but he considered her like a second mom to him and his mother. She'd greet them every morning with treats, water, hay or grain. She'd brush them down and watch as Surprise played. Even Surprise and the dog became friends. The dog would sneak under the corral fence and chase Surprise around the ring.

Word of a baby horse spread through the neighborhood. Kids and families would show up to lean on the corral fence, reaching out their tiny fingers to pet the soft, fuzzy nose of Surprise. *Little people like me!* he thought excitedly. Sometimes they fed him carrots or apples – his favorite. He learned about his surroundings – the two-legged creatures were considered "humans" or "people". Surprise enjoyed all the attention – the pats on the nose, the treats, the laughter. However, as with any young animal, all the attention made Surprise tired. He'd curl up in the hay in the barn to rest, away from prying eyes and dirty fingers.

*****

Weeks turned into months; months turned into years. Six years passed. Surprise was no longer that little colt with silky, black fur. He grew into his slick white and gray speckled adult coat. At full height, he wasn't quite as tall as his mother; his height qualified him as a pony in the world of equestrian standards. This news intrigued the children even more, often excited to visit the suburb's very own pony. Surprise didn't understand all this enthusiasm, but he certainly loved the attention. And just as the children watched Surprise grow, he watched them grow too. The young children were now teenagers and some of the previous teens moved off to school or now have babies of their own that they bring to visit Surprise. In his little suburb, he was a celebrity.

Surprise knew almost everyone. It was rare that a new face would come to the corral, unless they were accompanied by another local. Often the local would say "See, I told you we had horses in our suburbs. And this one is a pony," as they pointed to Surprise. He never had to worry about a stranger. He never met a human he didn't like. But one day, a stranger's visit changed his life forever.

"Well, Mary, here is our pony, Surprise" said Surprise's second mom, or as he liked to call her "his human".

I guess that new human is Mary. Surprise lifted his nose to the air to get a better view.

"Yeah! We'll take him," said Mary patting the corral fence. "Surprise will work in our group. He's at the age he needs to be trained; without proper care and training, male ponies or horses can be a bit aggressive," said Mary, squinting her eyes against the sun's direct rays.

Take me? Take me where? Surprise twitched his ears forward in wonder. After a few minutes of conversation, the women walked away, their hair waving in the breeze. Surprise was still curious and kept watching but when they were finally out of view, he went back to eating his hay.

Several minutes later, he heard a large creaking and rumbling noise. Generally, a rumbling noise like that meant more hay was arriving to

8

the barn. But this was new, and the creaking was louder than the rumble. Surprise lifted his head again, getting a better view of a large contraption nearing the corral. *What is this?* Surprise twitched his ears back. He started to back up toward the barn, spooked by the trailer that was coming toward their gate.

The women gathered around the back of the trailer, opened the door, lowered the ramp, then finally added feed and hay to the inside-front of the trailer. Surprise anxiously watched, twitching his ears back and forth with the new noises. *I do not like this.* Surprise snorted, widening his nostrils to show his irritation.

"Surprise, it's time for a new home," said his human, as she approached him from across the corral. "You'll have new friends and a bigger space. You'll love it!" She slowly led him to the trailer ramp, pausing so that he could smell the trailer and absorb his surroundings. *I don't know about this,* he thought.

She pulled out some of his favorite treats, including real apple slices. She stepped a few feet forward onto the trailer ramp. Surprise stretched out his neck to get a bite, but she was too far away. "Come on, Surprise," she coaxed. He took one step forward onto the trailer ramp and she rewarded him with an apple slice. She gave him a minute to chew. She took another two steps back, held out her hand again, letting Surprise smell another apple slice.

What is this game you're playing? Surprise thought, eyes scanning the trailer in front of him.

Surprise tried to take a bite of the next apple slice but again could not reach. He took another step forward. She took another step back. He took another step forward, this time he was fully standing on the trailer ramp. She rewarded him again. He fully trusted her. After all, she's been taking care of him and his mother all these years.

"Just a few more steps, boy," she said again, holding the slices in her hand. Finally, he was fully in the trailer. Fresh hay awaited him like a reward at the end of a race. "I will miss you, Surprise." She patted his head one last time and walked off the trailer. Surprise didn't understand this emotion that came from his human.

The trailer gate loudly clanked shut, with the latch giving a final snap of *wake up* to Surprise. *Wait — where's Mom?* Surprise looked out through the trailer bars, now realizing everything he knew was going to change. He continued to look around him in the trailer. It was just him. *WHERE'S MOM?* he shouted in his head. He started to pace the trailer, seeing his mother still in the corral. She marched back and forth, whinnying in protest as well. *Son, be brave, my son!* It was if she knew this day would come. *Be brave? Be brave for what?* he snorted back.

The trailer jerked into motion, making Surprise lose his footing. He stumbled to regain his balance. He watched his mother and his human slowly float away. The truck turned onto the street, pulling the trailer in a new direction. For those last few seconds, time stopped. The final image of them branded in his mind forever. His heart shattered into pieces of fear, anger, and sadness. Some of these emotions he had never felt before and didn't understand them.

Houses flashed by as the trailer rocked in rhythm with the truck speed. Surprise's panic and anxiety escalated. For the first time in his life, he felt alone. *Where am I going? Why me? Why isn't my mother coming with me?* He paced from one side of the trailer to the other, terrified of the fast-changing scenery. *Take me back now!*

PATIENCE IS A VIRTUE

By the time Surprise arrived at his new barn, his emotions were raw. He experienced so many negative emotions during the trip it felt as if his soul would just vanish into thin air. His desire for learning new things was no longer a flame in his heart. He didn't want new. He didn't want uncertainty like this. *Please, just take me back,* he pleaded over and over, not sure who was listening anymore. He was so focused on the negative feelings and fear that he didn't even realize that the trailer stopped moving.

Abruptly a loud clank snapped Surprise back into reality. Mary opened the trailer gates, talking softly to Surprise. "Hey buddy – welcome to your new home!". He watched her from the corner of his eye, *this isn't my home.* The sight of Mary agitated him. She was the reason he was no longer home. She was the reason for this unwanted, unvoiced change.

He watched her walk away from the trailer, leaving the gate wide open. Surprise stared at it. *Do I stay here? Do I go out?* After several minutes of looking around, assessing his current situation, he finally decided to get out. *This thing is a trap!* He approached the trailer gate with caution, stopping before his hooves could touch the ground. He stretched his neck and nose out into the air and smelled whiffs of other horses, hay, and humans. The frustration of the trailer and the move leaked into vague curiosity as he saw other horses nearby grazing on hay. Off to the side Mary spoke to another human. He strolled carefully down the ramp, but eager to leave the metal contraption behind him. Unfortunately, there was a gate between him and the other horses; but, directly in front of him was a prepped stall – hay, water, feed – no different than his previous home. Exhausted from the move, he hung his head and walked into the stall. A stall was his safe place back home. Perhaps it can be here too.

Mary's presence was consistent each day, but Surprise was too upset to eat or interact with her. He was so homesick, his chest felt heavy with longing of his old home. *Take me back,* he pleaded with Mary, praying she could hear his thoughts. *Mama, I'm trying to be brave. Is this what you meant?*

But Mary was patient. Every day, he watched as she fed him and groomed him. She gave him the time he needed to process his first move. After a few days, Surprise's appetite slowly returned. After a couple of weeks, his curiosity of the world around him began to liven his movements. Mary took this as a cue that it was time for training.

First day of training, Mary showed up to the stall as she did every day. This time, she brought a halter with her. She hung it in his stall, right next to his feed bucket. Mary knew that Surprise was a curious pony. She knew that he would notice something new in his stall. As she groomed him, she watched as Surprise sniffed at it.

Surprise's nostrils flared, smelling the musty scent of the tightly woven thread. The loose threads tickled his nose. *I can't eat this,* Surprise said disappointed. *What is this?*

As Mary groomed Surprise, she watched him assess the new addition to his stall. After time passed, she removed it from the hook. She held it at the edge of her fingertips slowly turning it in front of him.

"Surprise, this is a halter. You'll need to learn to wear this so that we can start to train you in many other things. But this is first," she confidently explained.

Surprise backed away. *I don't like that.* Mary just stood there, not approaching him yet. He reached his nose out to sniff it again, nostrils flaring wider. Then he yanked his head back, his mane flopping heavily against his neck. *Nope.*

Mary approached Surprise, petting his back, halter still in hand. As she petted him, she slowly slipped the halter over his nose then loosely hooked the top of it over his ears, letting it sit there. It wasn't snug, just…there. It was a new sensation for Surprise, his ears twitched in a mixture of frustration and wonder. *She may be nice…*his thoughts trailed off to distant feelings. *I'm still leery of her.*

After a couple of minutes, Mary decided that the day's lesson was done. "You did good!" she said, pulling out some apple snacks for him. She slipped off the halter over his ears, then his nose. As Mary gathered her things to leave, Surprise watched her closely, processing this new activity she just introduced. *Why did she do that? What "training" is she talking about?* he pondered.

It's not that bad once you get used to it said a voice on the other side of his stall. Surprise was – well – surprised – to hear from another horse. Often, horses don't chat with each other verbally, they use their movements and touches to communicate with each other. But considering there was a stall between them, that kind of communication was difficult.

I'm sorry – what? Surprise responded.

Mary is good. A new place is hard but know that you are welcomed here. Trust me when I say, it will get easier, the voice charmed. Surprise couldn't see his neighbor. *By the way, they call me Honey Girl.*

Surprise didn't say anything. He was still shy and a little skeptical of some of this new activity, as well as this other horse that seemed to be brainwashed.

*****

The next day, Mary showed up with the same halter. Surprise was not amused. *Uh…I said no yesterday,* Surprise reminded her. But Mary didn't seem to know or understand what he was saying because she continued with her routine. This time, she slipped on the halter in one swift movement before Surprise knew what was happening. Mary left no room for yesterday's sniff test. *No.* He shook his head, trying to shake it off. More snacks for positive reinforcement.

Next day, same routine.

After a couple of days, Surprise automatically dipped his nose into the halter when she presented it. *Ok, fine,* he thought, standing quietly as Mary buckled the halter behind his ears to keep it in place.

"That a boy!" exclaimed Mary. She gave him extra treats for the win.

See – told you! said Honey Girl. Slowly she and Surprise became friends. Surprise needed her coaching and "grown up" tough love to work through some of his anxiety of the new barn and new routines. Mary finally allowed Surprise to visit the pasture where Surprise got to see Honey Girl's chestnut, honey-colored fur shining in the bright sun. Surprise was in awe of her.

Mary continued similar training tactics to prepare him for trail riding such as saddling, bits, rein training, and finally rider dynamics. Each new lesson, Honey Girl was there to talk him through it. Mary treated him with real apple slices for continued positive progress. After several months, Mary managed to work with Surprise enough to get him comfortable with trail riding. Mary's patience and soft ways gave Surprise the room he needed to adjust. He learned to trust her and although he still missed his first home, this place had a newness to it that made it exciting for his young heart.

When Mary wasn't around, he was never alone. His home was a larger barn with other horses and other humans who cared for them or used them to train riders. Surprise anxiously awaited the days' activities of horse and rider training.

Honey Girl's owner or "human" was Missy. Although Missy could train just about anyone of any age, her specialty was teaching young riders. Everyday Missy and her children would come to visit the barn. Her children would visit or ride Surprise while Missy used Honey Girl for riding lessons with students. And while Missy was busy with Honey Girl, she knew that her children were safe with Surprise because of his sweet, gentle nature.

"Surprise!" Missy's children would excitedly yelled out while they climbed into this stall. They'd start to tell Surprise about their day. "Today was awesome! We got to watch a movie for history class."

Hey guys, Surprise thought. *So glad to see you!* He swished his tail in excitement.

As Missy's kids visited Surprise, Missy went into training mode with her student. Her passion for horses and students were a marvel for Surprise to watch. "Did you know that if you feed a horse too much, it could be deadly?" The student's eyes widened with wonderment and shook her head no. "Yeah, it's true! Horses can't burp or throw up like us humans can. So, if they eat too much or if they eat something that gives them gas in their belly, it can kill them! That's why it is always important to ask the owner of the horse if it is ok to feed them and more importantly, what to feed them." The student nodded in compliance.

Well, that explains why people stop giving me snacks. Surprise amused himself, twitching his ears forward to listen more.

*****

Missy and Mary were very good friends. Often when Missy wasn't teaching, she and Mary would take Honey Girl and Surprise on trail rides. These were more relaxed times, just living in the moment – no riding lessons, no other humans, just the four friends. Surprise was very comfortable on the trail rides; he knew when to jump, when to step around or over a rock. Mary completely trusted her pony and Surprise completely trusted her direction. This was all thanks to her patience and training abilities.

Surprise studied Honey Girl's and Missy's methods for trail riding. He watched Honey Girl carefully place her hooves around larger rocks, roots, or holes. He'd listen to Missy's tone of voice with Honey Girl as they crossed more difficult spots on the trails, then equally watch Missy's movements to match the needs of Honey Girl as she navigated the path. As he was caught up in his thoughts, it dawned on him how much he has grown since his move. He was no longer that scared, little pony. He became a trained, brave trail rider! *Ma, if only you could see me now!* he would brag, ignoring the distant pain of missing her.

Back in the stable, he and Honey Girl would swap stories from their ride or from their past. One day Surprise shared the story of how he got his name.

So there I was, this tiny, scared baby and the woman had no idea that my mother was pregnant! How does that even happen? Surprise laughed.

Oh, that's just precious, she said. *And scary! Imagine if that jogger didn't find you! Well, pretty sure my name is because of the color of my coat. A little more boring than your story,* Honey Girl snorted.

*****

The move to this new place was now a distant memory. The years mended his heart as he learned to trust and love Mary, Missy, Honey Girl, and many of the other humans that came to visit. The bittersweet memories of his birth mother and first human mother were locked away in his heart. He now understood that his journey was necessary. It wasn't easy. Surprise often reminisced about the move, Mary's training, his first trail ride, and first meeting Honey Girl. All of it was so new, so scary, so aggravating, so...annoying. The fear of moving again lingered like a dark shadow in the back of his mind. But he didn't dawdle on these thoughts knowing that it will make him spiral into paranoia. He would force those thoughts aside and focus on the present moment with his friends – both human and equine. *Yes,* he sighs, *this is now my home.*

One morning Surprise ate his breakfast as Mary attended his stall, laying new straw to the floor for his comfort and cleanliness. He could hear Honey Girl in the next stall, slopping at her water. As his ears twitched to the typical morning noises, a new noise interrupted – and his heart froze in fear. *Did I just hear what I heard? Or did I make that up in my head?* Surprise wondered. His ears twitched again, and he became very still. Water slopping, pitchfork scraping the floor, the hay rustling, near-by snorting of another horse, and a creak. *Yes! There it is again!*

Soon the creaking covered all stall noises then changed into moaning and rumbling. Memories from his first move flooded into his head, his heart drummed heavily in his chest, ears twitched in anticipation. Suddenly, there it was – the trailer, *the trap! I remember what happened last time I saw one of those.* And although he loved his life now, it was not an easy transition for him. Surprise shrunk into the furthest corner of his stall, regressing into that young pony several years ago.

Missy came into the stall with him. "Well sweet boy, it's time to say good-bye." She gently patted his forehead. "We're moving. You've been a blessing to Honey Girl and our family. We will miss you dearly."

Missy's voice was different; she seemed…sad. As Surprise listened, he realized that it wasn't him moving. It was his friend, Honey Girl!

"Honey Girl will be going to a new home with more room and my family is moving north," Missy said, handing Surprise an apple snack. The shrieks of Missy's kids got louder as they approached his stall. "Surprise!" they said, hugging on his front shoulder and neck. "We'll miss you so much!"

I've never heard their voices this way before. Surprise sensed their sadness. He turned his head to the girl and rubbed her back with his nose. He quivered his lip against her shirt, pulling her toward him more. As they slipped away, Missy moved over to Honey Girl's stall.

What did they just say? Honey Girl asked in a panic.

Surprise was too stunned to say anything. A part of him was relieved it wasn't him getting on that trap of a trailer. But the other part of him ached for his friend. The ache and the relief swirled like a cyclone in his heart.

No, I don't want to go! Honey Girl pleaded. *You are my humans! I love you all!*

Although Missy and the kids couldn't hear Honey Girl's plea, Missy assured her that she was going to a good home. A new, bittersweet relief came over Surprise. Now it was Surprise's turn to comfort Honey Girl.

Honey Girl, I know this is hard. But you know Missy will ensure you have a safe, happy home. You will be happy again, Surprise whispered to his friend. He was panicked but wanted to be strong for his friend. He wished he could move through the stall wall to nuzzle with her.

Honey Girl fell silent as Missy and the kids moved around the stall, picking up buckets, cleaning out the hay, and softly saying good-byes. Mary moved over to Honey Girl's stall to help Missy. The air was thick with tense feelings. Surprise paced his stall, wishing he could do something to change Missy's mind.

Just then, Surprise saw Missy walk by his stall, then the lead rope, then Honey Girl's beautiful face inched into view. As she walked past, her eyes met his and the sadness and loneliness in her eyes reflected how he felt. *Will I ever see her again? Will I ever see the kids again?*

And just like that, they were gone.

AN OLD FRIEND RETURNS

Mary kept Surprise busy with trail riding over the next several weeks and months. During the rides, he felt the void of Missy and Honey Girl's absence. He'd shift his thoughts to the trail and methodically concentrate on every step, every stone, every branch in his path. But in the evening when the ride was hours past, the people were gone, and the barn was still, Surprise felt alone. His thoughts would roll back into time where he and Honey Girl talked or grunted between dinner bites. He remembered all their conversations and laughs. Now it was quiet except for the echoes in his memory. Indeed, he missed his friend.

As months passed, the sting of Honey Girl's absence began to dull. He would often think about his days of leaving his original barn and then Honey Girl leaving. *Perhaps this is the life of a horse?* he pondered. *We just go where the humans take us.* He concluded. *'Be brave,' my mother told me.* He continued to analyze his life and recent events. The humans he encountered so far have been very kind, but he doesn't understand the need to move. *How can we tell them we don't want to move?*

Just as months had passed, so did the years. Missy and Honey Girl became a distant memory. Surprise got used to the new horses in the barn. He would recognize when a new horse needed a friend. The new horse's eyes were often wide in fear and ears were stretched back in confusion. In those moments, Surprise remembered himself in that way but also remembered how Honey Girl welcomed him. Now it was Surprise's turn to pay the kindness forward.

*****

One day Mary prepared Surprise for another trail ride but this time, she hummed while brushing him. His ears perked at the pleasant sound. *This is new,* he thought. He watched her from the corner of his eye. She seemed very lost in thought. *Why does she keep rubbing her belly like that?* he wondered. Little did Surprise know, Mary was pregnant.

As the weeks passed, Surprise watched as Mary's belly grew. Although the change was gradual, he could tell something special was happening to her. Sometimes she was a little slower to finish the feeding routine. She'd lean back a little further with her hand in the small of her back. Some days, she'd breathe a little harder, resting on top of a feed bucket. As her belly grew larger, her routines were slower.

One evening Mary came into his stall, brushing his back as he ate his hay. She started to hum the same song she always did; Surprise's ears twitched to the lullaby. Her peaceful mood and humming caressed Surprise's soul.

"Well sweet boy, we've had some great times together," Mary said, rubbing her belly as she brushed his back. "But, just as my life is changing, so will yours."

What does that mean? Surprise twitched his ears back. Mary continued to hum. The night was calm, the mood serene. *What did she mean that my life will be changing?* he kept thinking.

Mary seemed to be in a trance, humming, brushing…humming, brushing. Sometimes she'd brush the same spot for several minutes before moving to another spot on Surprise's back. She'd rest for a few minutes, then stand up and brush him some more. Surprise's eyes drooped as she continued her lullaby. Her comment faded away like a dream. Soon Surprise drifted to sleep.

The next day, Surprise woke up to a familiar voice in the distance. "I could not believe that the ad for a pony was yours, Mary! Here, after all this time has passed, the exact pony my family grew to love is for sale at the same time I'm looking for a large pony to train younger students. I mean, could the stars be any more aligned?" the voice chuckled.

Surprise twitched his ears forward, listening intently. *Is that...* he asked himself. He flared his nostrils out as he could smell her familiar scent as she approached his stall. *It has to be!* he assumed. Suddenly, there she was in front of him. Surprise excitedly bumped his head against his old friend, flopping his mane in delight.

"Oh, you sweet boy! We've missed you!" said Missy, handing him an apple snack.

After hugs, pats, kisses on Surprise's nose, and more treats, Missy slipped a halter onto his head. *Oh, how I've missed you!* Surprise gladly accepted the halter, expecting a routine trail ride to start. But as she led him around the barn and out of the corral, he saw it. A trailer. He immediately stiffened.

Is this what Mary meant last night? Surprise remembered Mary's comment. Although he was very happy to see Missy, the good vibes started to fade as he stared at the moving cage. *If I go, will I see Honey Girl?* he hoped. But then he remembered that Missy said she was going to a new home. *So no.* he calculated. He lifted his head in frustration. *Humans just take us where they want us.*

"Come on boy, it's ok," said Missy. Surprise completely trusted Missy for all the years she worked with him. By now, at the age of 17,

Surprise was the most gentle and trustworthy pony that Missy knew. But just as Surprise gained her trust over the years, it is now her turn to gain his trust again. She allowed him to pause and sniff the trailer. She walked in front of him, up the ramp, and held out

Surprise (later to be named "Sir Prize") and Missy

her hand. Surprise sniffed her hand, realizing she had treats. "Come on boy, you can do this." She walked back a few feet and then paused.

Surprise followed a few steps. *I trust you but I still don't like this* he thought. Before he made his final steps into the trailer, he turned his head to the barn and corral he's known as home for the last several years. He knew what was coming. *I may never see this place again. Mary, the students, all of them. Don't I get to say good-bye?* With a sigh of defeat, he turned back to look inside the trailer. *Fine. But only because it's you, Missy.* And with a sad heart and a lot of faith, he followed Missy completely into the trailer.

"Remember, he doesn't like to be tied up," Mary warned. "We kept trying to teach him that being tied up is safe, but he never learned to like it."

Surprise heard this and laughed to himself. *This is true. I accepted everything else, but do not tie the lead rope to another object that doesn't move. It's a hard no for me.*

"Well, I don't want there to be any issues during travel. I'd prefer to tie him," Missy stated as she knotted the rope to a ring in the trailer. Surprise stood listening to their banter then shook his head as if to say no, flopping his mane in disbelief.

Mary shrugged her shoulders and laughed, "Well, he does look calm. And maybe he's ok with your bigger trailer than my small one."

Surprise stood there stunned. *Did she not just tell you to not tie me?* Missy got into her truck to take Surprise to his new home. The trailer slowly rocked back and forth as she picked up speed on the road. *You know, it's bad enough I'm in this trailer that I don't like in the first place. But then you must tie me too? Even after Mary told you not to do it! This is unacceptable.* Surprise pulled on the rope in defiance. He didn't care that the halter buckle pinched him behind his ears. He didn't care that the ring of the halter dug into his cheek. He simply did not want to be tied. *I need to move. I need to roam. This won't let me.* Surprise fought the rope like an angry badger.

Finally, Surprise just flopped on the trailer floor. The rope was still tied to his halter, forcing his head to hang at an odd angle against the trailer wall. His breathing was labored, but he didn't care. *I said no. This will teach you to listen to me!* he argued silently. The heavy force from Surprise's protest vibrated through the trailer into the truck. Missy could tell something was wrong as the truck's axles shivered in response.

"What in the world?" she sighed out loud. She pulled over to check on Surprise. As she walked to the back of the trailer, she could not see him through the trailer side windows. "Odd," she whispered under her breath. She opened the trailer gate slowly, expectations as shaky as the truck's previous movement. Her eyes widened in shock. "Oh my gosh!" she gasped. She pulled out her pocketknife and immediately cut the rope free.

Surprise's head relaxed from the tangled strain. For a moment, he just stayed on the floor. He then awkwardly stood, shaking his head to readjust the halter on his nose. Now that he was more relaxed, he turned his head to look at Missy, nodding several times, hair flopping around his eyes. *See. They told you not to tie me.* He looked at Missy with stubbornness, nose quivering with humor.

"Well, you sly little…," Missy laughed as she untied the remaining rope from the trailer ring. "Smart. Ok, have it your way." She walked off the trailer, locking the door behind her. As she passed the trailer side windows, she peaked in to look at Surprise. He watched her with those smug eyes. Missy walked away, shaking her head in disbelief.

Surprise heard the truck door close, then felt the gentle rock of movement again. *At least I'm not tied up anymore. I won this battle.*

A KNIGHTED PONY

Missy backed the trailer against a corral fence. After Missy settled Surprise into her barn, she looked out to her corral with joy and content. She watched as Surprise walked the corral, checking out his new home. Her business of training horses and students grew significantly but it wasn't complete without a pony. And she was blessed that Surprise was now officially a part of her family.

She loved horses since she was a kid, ever since she saw a picture of her grandfather sitting on a large, magnificent horse named Jackatar. She fondly remembered her days at horse camp where she learned to horseback ride, how to take care of a horse, and studied the different breeds of horses.

Her life-long love of horses became her career. Missy managed a local horse barn as well as had her own riding lessons company, using many of the residential horses for riding lessons. And Surprise, the pony, was the special addition to her horse family that would expand her teachings to children or small adults.

As Missy reminisced and felt accomplished, Surprise studied his new home. *Looks clean.* He walked to the stalls to observe the other horses. *Hi. I'm new.* The other horses cautiously watched their new barn mate from a distance. Surprise nodded, *yep, I know. Change is hard.* Surprise continued his discovery slowly and methodically, having small talks with the other horses that were willing to chat.

Later that evening Missy came to visit Surprise during her feeding routine. But she wasn't alone. "Come on, Chap," Missy said, talking to a small, black and white dog. He had small black eyes that were friendly and welcoming. His fur was long and seemed soft, but of course Surprise made this assumption from his limited engagement with previous dogs. Chap followed at her heels and went wherever she did. He walked right into Surprise's stall as if it were his home too. He gently walked toward Surprise and sniffed his front hooves. Surprise bent his head down, flared out his nostrils, and sniffed the top of Chap's head. Chap looked up and licked his nose as if to say "Welcome!" Surprise took this as a good sign. *Well, at least I made one new friend.*

Missy waited no time putting Surprise to work training students. It was just like old times between Surprise and Missy. He knew what to expect and so did she. Other than the place and horses being new, Surprise was relieved for the familiarity of his old friend. Plus, he looked forward to Chap's presence every day as well.

As the days and weeks passed, Missy repeated her animal care lessons to newer or younger students. "Did you know that if a horse eats too much, it could be fatal?" Missy explained while feeding oats to Surprise. The kids' eyes were wide in wonder, slowly shaking their heads in disbelief. "Yeah! I must be especially careful to not leave buckets of feed out overnight or he'd eat it all! It would give him a horrible stomachache. Those hurt, don't they?" The kids nodded. Surprise nodded too, knocking the bucket out of her hand. After all, if he distracted Missy enough, he could eat more. The children enjoyed the show, shrilling with laughter.

Missy continued to tell stories about Surprise. "Horses and ponies are also known as equines. Equines are measured in hands," Missy explained to her students, shifting her hands up Surprise's legs and shoulders to count. "If they measured around 14 hands tall or less, then it is considered a pony, like Surprise. But if the equine is 14 hands or taller," again Missy shifted her hands up over Surprise's shoulders, "then it is a horse."

"So...he's not a horse?" one student asked, pointing to Surprise.

"Nope. He is not," Missy stated.

Surprise just listened, always learning from Missy as she taught others. *Huh...so that's why they call me a pony. I find her information so interesting!*

She was not only a natural with Surprise but all horses and animals. But even more, Surprise witnessed how Missy's eyes sparkled when she taught children how to ride. He used Missy's cues on when to turn, when to stop, when to go, when to slow down, when to speed up, and when to jump. Their trust in each other grew deeper every day. And with their adventures, Chap was always right there with them, chasing squirrels or rabbits along the way.

After a rider learned the basics of horse riding in the corral, Missy would advance them to trail riding or jumping lessons. The trail was full of hills, valleys, rocks, a small creek, and various terrain options. This environment challenged the rider to anticipate the horse's or pony's body movements. It became a dance of trust. It required the rider to learn to trust the animal's judgement on the speed and accuracy of where to step. The rider also would learn to respond to the needs of the animal to ensure safety for not only the rider, but also the animal.

One day, Missy prepared a student for a trail ride lesson. Although Surprise was very used to the trail, he sensed the girl's anxiety.

"Are you sure we're ready for this?" the girl asked.

"Of course!" Missy said "You have nothing to worry about. Surprise and I are a team and we've done this many times. You will be fine. Just remember, use the reins to tell Surprise where you want to go but let him do the work."

The girl nodded and shifted her weight in the saddle. Surprise twitched his ears forward, anxious for the trail. It was a favorite of his. He knew where all the rocks were, all the limbs, all the holes…everything. He could walk that trail blindfolded and still get home before feeding time. But more importantly, his comfort level with the trail was because of his trust in Missy. His connection to Missy was like that of a child to their mother. He and Missy were remarkably close; this helped them build riding confidence in the riders. *Don't worry, kid. I got you.* Surprise adjusted the bit in his mouth. *I'm ready to go!* Chap was yards ahead, sniffing out the trail.

The four started the trail ride, no different than any other time. Missy walked beside Surprise and the rider, giving instructions to the young girl. "You see this hill coming, make sure you lean forward a little to help with Surprise's balance." She continued with additional instructions of how to lean back when going down a hill or gently standing when Surprise jumped over objects. "When you learn to move with him, this reduces the chances of injury to him."

They progressed into the trail when they came across another group of riders. Missy stopped their lessons briefly to talk to them; the girl patiently waited in Surprise's saddle. While the humans chatted, there seemed to be a stare down between the other, much larger horses and Surprise. While he took in their muscular, towering builds, they peered down their noses at his much smaller stature. Surprise felt uneasy at the judgmental stares.

Suddenly, a large truck rumbled by on the road near the trail. The loud noise frightened one of the horses in the other group. He reared onto his hind legs, slinging his rider to the ground. The horse ran past the other horses, startling them too. They became frantic and accidently bumped into each other. A few bucked, kicking their strong back legs into the air. Another rider fell to the ground. It was chaos! Even Chap walked backwards away from all the activity, unsure what to expect.

"Missy!" the girl cried out from the saddle. Surprise anxiously twitched his ears back. Missy quickly called to her "Shorten your reins!" Then she looked at Surprise "Easy, Surprise! Take it easy!" The student was so scared which made Surprise nervous.

I've never seen this much excitement before. Surprise shifted his eyes between the other horses. *What do I do?* His ears twitched forward then backward, listening to the other horses and Missy. He shuffled his legs and weight in anticipation of what to do next. Everyone was scared!

Surprise thought about the situation, almost in slow motion. In the past, he relied on his rider, or his trainer Missy, to handle challenging situations. But now, the girl was undecisive and frightened. He had never been in a position where he had to take the lead from the rider. *Is that even a thing? Can I do that?* He thought back to all of his days of training. *Missy or Mary told the rider what to do. The rider then told me what to do. But this time, the rider isn't doing giving any direction.* He pondered what to do; the madness continued to unfold in front of him: Missy sternly but calmly coaxed Surprise and the rider, the other riders grabbed at their agitated horses.

The girl did not shorten her reins; she was paralyzed with fear from watching other riders fall off their horses. She clearly didn't know what to do. But Surprise finally did. *I need to focus on Missy.* He shifted his ears toward Missy, listening to her voice, and walked calmly across the path. As he reached Missy, he leaned his head against her.

Surprise started to think *These horses are crazy! Is it OK if I just stand here, with you?* In that moment, Missy knew that Surprise was different from other horses. He was completely connected to her and her lead, not influenced by other actions around him.

Missy guided them away from the other horse group and found a private spot on the trail to check in on the student. "You ok?" Missy asked the student. She nodded slowly. Surprise could feel her shaking through the saddle; her anxiety spiked after that event.

First day on the trail and this happened! Poor thing! Surprise empathized; he too had never experienced this. He twitched his ears back and forth, listening for the other horses to come galloping by them. The trail was silent other than their breathing and talking.

Missy gave them all a minute to catch their breath and calm down. "You know what's interesting, I've never seen Surprise do that before," she told the student. "If you think about what the other horses were doing and what Surprise did, that's really a good thing." Surprise listened to Missy's assessment of what happened. "It is unusual for a horse to remain calm in something like that. And Surprise did!" She leaned over and patted Surprise on the nose and smiled up at the girl. "It may have been a rough start to your trail riding, but this was a very good lesson in trust." Surprise sensed the girl's new calmness as Missy praised his actions.

When they got back to the barn, the girl unsaddled Surprise, brushed him, and thanked him for not bucking her off his back. Just before she left, she asked Missy "Is it ok if I write a thank you letter to Surprise and draw a picture of him?"

Missy grinned and said, "Of course! Surprise would love that!"

The girl smiled wide, patted his neck again, and fed him his favorite apple snacks. She stopped and looked at Missy. "How do you spell his name?"

Missy thought about it for a while. She leaned down and whispered "You know. After what we saw today. I think his name should be spelled special, like him. His name is now two words. Sir Prize. 'Sir' is a title for bravery. And he is the best prize in the world. So, his name is Sir Prize. S-I-R P-R-I-Z-E." And just like that, Surprise was knighted as Sir Prize.

FROM WEST TO MID-WEST

Missy's corral in southern California was in "horse paradise", just a half mile from the beach. The western winds carried the ocean scent across the sandy floors of the corral. It was mild year-round with a few rain showers in the winter months, but all in all Sir Prize loved it there. The soil was mostly sand which was great for him to lie on his back, awkwardly wiggle around to scratch that one hard-to-reach itchy spot. Sometimes he'd lie on his belly for a good belly scratch. The kids would laugh and point he would rock back and forth on the sand, rubbing his belly against the sandy ground. He loved hearing their laughs.

Trail rides included riding along the beach, sandy trails, and small sand dunes. Sunset beach rides were Sir Prize's favorite. The water would reach out and tease his hooves before it was sucked back into the vast ocean. The sun would set low in the horizon, giving an orange glow across water, and stretching their shadows into taller, thinner versions of themselves. The breeze provided protection from any flies or bugs. Indeed, Sir Prize grew to love this home. After all, experiencing the beach almost every day was a dream come true that he didn't know existed!

However, as beautiful as it was, the horses did not have a pasture to graze on grass. Missy would have regular shipments of hay come to the barn to ensure that Sir Prize and his barn roommates had something to eat between grain feeds. After all, as they say, "Hay is for horses"! Sir Prize was used to grazing on hay so he didn't know or understand the delicacy of dining on fresh grass like many other horses do. And in Sir

Missy riding Sir Prize near the beach

Prize's current world, he was just as happy with a sandy beach and imported hay.

Seasons and students came and went. Sir Prize was content in his southern California home. Although he made other horse friends, he was closest to Missy and Chap. His routine consisted of morning feedings, stall cleaning, new student training, trail riding, jump training, more feeding, and corral free time.

If his routine changed, it made him nervous. He'd anxiously pace the corral until Missy came. *She should be here by now.*

"I know, I know, I'm late," she would say. "I'm right here. You're fine." And just like that, Sir Prize would be back to his calm self.

*****

One morning, Missy arrived at the barn earlier than normal. She moved things around - the buckets, the feed, and the hay to outside the corral. Sir Prize saw this and realized it was not part of the normal routine. He pranced to the other side of the corral, twitching his ears forward. *What is happening?*

Suddenly there was a large truck and a trailer backing up to the barn. Sir Prize watched with an intense stare, twitching his ears back as the truck and trailer creaked and squeaked into place.

Oh no. Not again. He snorted through his nostrils, frustrated with the pending activities. *Why do they keep moving me? Why do they make me leave? What have I done that they don't want me anymore?* Sir Prize was now angry, pacing faster on the far fence of the corral.

"Just park it here," Missy said. She started to load the buckets, feed, and hay into the trailer. Sir Prize saw his apple snacks bucket also go into the trailer. His ears perked, nostrils flared, lips twitched. He pawed at the ground, nervous from all the commotion in front of him.

Missy walked toward Sir Prize, halter in hand. She patted his neck and whispered "You're going on an adventure, my friend. I need you to trust me." She slid the halter over his head as Chap ran up next to him. She was calm and Chap didn't leave his side; Sir Prize started to relax. She stood with Sir Prize for a few minutes, talked to him in a gentle tone. "I have a few of your favorite snacks," she opened her hand. Sir Prize wiggled his lips over her hand to accept the gift.

She slowly walked Sir Prize toward the trailer, pausing at the ramp to let him take his time to inspect the large contraption. He leaned his head down and sniffed the ramp. He then lifted his head back up, wide-eyed at this large door in front of him.

Just then another lady appeared in front of Missy, Sir Prize, and Chap. "Well! It will be a long road ahead of him, but don't you worry, I will take good care of him," she said, dusting off her jeans.

Who. Is. This? Sir Prize enunciated every word in his head as if each word needed its own sentence. Sir Prize looked at Missy, then looked at this person. She was short, wearing dusty work clothes, weathered lines around her eyes. Her eyes sparkled with delight as she looked directly at Sir Prize.

"Well, aren't you a doll!" she said out loud, chuckling. She then looked at Missy and they started to chatter. Sir Prize hung on every word trying to understand the situation that was unfolding before him.

"I really appreciate your help. I have all my own belongings to move and unfortunately, I just can't take him with me directly," said Missy.

She doesn't even sound sad! Do I mean nothing to her that she's just handing me off to this…this…stranger? Sir Prize anxiously asked. He wanted to scream in human voice so much just to get their attention, but it was useless.

"I had to laugh when you said you wanted to rent room for three stalls. He must be special," said the new lady, raising an eyebrow at the custom order Missy must have made for Sir Prize.

Rent? What does "rent" mean? Sir Prize had never heard that word.

"Yes, well, we've learned the hard way that he does not like to be tied during transport. He'll do fine otherwise. And with it being such a long ride, I wanted to make it as comfortable as possible for him," explained Missy.

"Ok then! Let me show you what I've got and then we'll get him inside," said the new lady, stepping up into the trailer.

Missy disappeared with her. Sir Prize heard the faint creaking as their weight moved the trailer. The faint creak was just a reminder of the doom to come. Sir Prize despised this moment. The realization he will never be back here. Not once in his life did he ever move back to a place he lived and grew to love. *Not once,* he seethed.

Sir Prize was lost in his thoughts as the ladies came back to greet him.

Missy softly grabbed his halter and rubbed his nose. "Come on, boy, it will be alright," she calmly whispered into his ear. She walked a few feet in front of Sir Prize, held the rope in one hand and presented his favorite – apple snacks – in the other. He leaned his nose out to her hand for a bite, but she took a step back. Sir Prize followed. Soon, he was on the trailer where she wanted him, and she immediately fed him the snacks. *I always fall for this.*

As Sir Prize finished chewing his snack, his eyes widened at the inside of the trailer. Most trailers were baren, metal cages. Maybe they were painted, maybe they weren't. They were usually beat up with scratches and dents. After all, they were meant to move an animal, not meant to be a luxury hotel. *Not that I know what that is like,* he sarcastically thought. But this trailer – it was luxurious for a horse trailer.

The new lady must be the owner of this trailer. It was long, multiple stalls for multiple horses. The inside of the trailer was painted with a mural of pastures and skylines. Sir Prize never experienced anything like this. His stall was wider, just as they described. It was filled with bedding and hay, just waiting for Sir Prize's presence. For a minute he stopped chewing as he took in his accommodating surroundings. *What in the world?* he gaped.

"Good boy," Missy said. "I'll see you in a few days." She patted his back and walked out of the trailer. He heard the clanking of the doors shutting and he was immediately scared, ears twitching. "Oh, and notice I didn't tie you up this time," Missy grinned back at Sir Prize.

A few days? Wait – so you're NOT leaving me? I'm so confused. If you're not leaving me, then why am I moving again? I don't understand! If he could grab the trailer window bars with his hooves, he'd do it like an innocently jailed civilian. Through the windows he watched her leave, trailed by Chap. *Oh, he doesn't have to get in the trailer? Where are you going?*

*****

As the trailer creaked and shifted from the road divots, Sir Prize shifted his attention back to his surroundings. He was confused by this move. *She'll see me again? Fancy trailer? Rent – whatever that meant?* As he rattled off the list of things that didn't add up, he realized he wasn't alone on the trailer this time. *One more odd thing to add to my list.* Previously, he was the only horse in a much smaller trailer. This time, however, there were other horses along for the ride. His stall was wider, allowing him the ability to roam a few extra inches. All the other horses were tied to the rings in their stall. As he turned to look at them, they couldn't see him. He just saw a row of swishing tails.

Sir Prize watched landscapes change through the air holes of the trailer. He spent hours listening to the clanking of the metal, the roar of the truck engine, and feeling the breeze race through his mane.

After several hours on the road, the sun lowered onto the horizon. Previously, Sir Prize had not been in a trailer this big for this long. He felt unsettled. It was feeding time and he was ready to be off the trailer. Just as the stars peeked through the sky canvas, the trailer came to a stop near a barn. The inviting barn lights lit the dark sky. Humans actively cleaned stalls and fed other horses, as if working in a barn at night wasn't unusual.

Sir Prize heard the trailer doors squeak open. The same lady that talked to Missy earlier in the day appeared in front of him. *I never caught her name,* Sir Prize realized. She went straight to work walking the horses and Sir Prize off the trailer, one by one. She swiftly moved each of them into individual stalls in the brightly lit barn. None of the horses seemed concerned with this lady that was taking care of them. *Do they know her? Where is Missy?* he asked himself. *Is she my new human?* he softly questioned.

Sir Prize watched her go from stall to stall, carrying buckets of feed, water, and flakes of hay. He was so tired from the trailer ride, yet his

37

adrenaline was fighting the sleep that beckoned his eyelids. *Is this my new home?* he pondered. As the lady disappeared into one of the other stalls, Sir Prize took a quick look around him.

Well, it's clean, he observed. *And the rest of the barn seemed managed appropriately,* he critiqued. Sir Prize kept himself busy with analyzing every detail to avoid the exhaustion, the confusion, and the loneliness he was feeling. His ears twitched at each new noise. Anxiety climbed inside his chest.

Finally, the lady stopped in front of Sir Prize's stall. She held out her hand, presenting his favorite apple snacks. "Hey buddy," she said softly, her eyes were also weary from driving. "Missy told me trips make you uneasy. I promise to take good care of you until you get to your final destination."

Final destination? What does that mean? Is this not it? Sir Prize's eyes widened in disbelief. *Where am I going?* he screamed at her in his head. The lady was oblivious to Sir Prize's internal monologue as she added feed, water, and hay into his stall. Just the smell of the grain made Sir Prize's hunger override any exhaustion and anxiety he was feeling. He hastily dipped his nose into his feed bucket. *It still smells like my old barn,* he sighed briefly in peace.

*****

The next morning, the same lady greeted Sir Prize, gathering his feed, his hay, his snacks and put them into the same beautifully painted trailer. Her tanned, weathered face smiled softly as she coaxed Sir Prize back into his trailer stall. "I know, I know, you don't want to come back on, but look – I have snacks," she showed a pile of apple snacks just for Sir Prize. *Well, she's been nice so far. And she has snacks.* Sir Prize slowly walked to his dedicated space. He had room to turn around and watch her load the other horses. As they passed him, they didn't look at him, they didn't acknowledge him, just like the night before. *Well good morning to you too,* he mocked in his head. Considering they weren't being friendly he decided to turn and look through side openings of the trailer. He realized this position put his rear and tail in full view as they walked by his stall. *Isn't this the view you're expecting anyways?* he continued to mock. He wasn't feeling his best self that day. He was tired, wished Missy was there. He didn't want to be on the trailer again. *I mean, two days on a trailer? Never have I ever…* his thoughts drifted off as he realized the lady just closed the trailer gates. *I guess we're headed out now. Brace yourselves!* He blew air through his closed lips, making the ppppfffttt sound that the humans love so much. Soon the trailer groaned and clanked down the road.

This process repeated itself for a couple of nights. Sometimes she would stop in the middle of the day, allowing the horses to rest their legs from trailer fatigue. The lady never rushed. And of course, she treated Sir Prize with his apple snacks. It was a small taste of home in Missy's absence.

"I know this is not fun," she'd say. "But you'll be at your new home soon."

Another new home. Sir Prize cautiously thought. *Can't I just stay in one place for once? Where is Missy?* Sir Prize slowly chewed his snacks but hung his head low with sadness.

Never did Sir Prize stop wondering about Missy. He was confused, terrified, and furious. *How could she leave me like this?* he flared his nostrils. *Why am I not home? Where am I going? Will I ever get off this thing? Where is Missy?* Sir Prize swirled in these thoughts as the trailer traveled for miles on the roads. Just thinking of Missy made his heart ache with loneliness and frustration. *How could she put me in this moving, metal semblance of a barn?* he pawed at the floor. *I'm tired of moving to new places with new people and new horses.*

*****

Sir Prize lost count of the days he was on the trailer. He didn't understand time the way humans did; but he understood night and day, sunrise and sunset. There were routines to consider. Suddenly, his routine was based upon what time they loaded onto or off of the trailer. He knew the lady was very nice, knew horses, and in all reality, he felt a bond with her. But he still missed Missy. He wanted to "just be" in his barn, his corral.

As he rocked back and forth from the trailer's road surfing, he stared into the distance. He wasn't concentrating on the outside world. His emotions were numb, and he was in a state of "whatever". He tried not to think of Missy because it would just bring back a wave of emotions that he was too exhausted to mend. The scenery turned from highway to big buildings with big windows to houses. *Wait – houses?* He perked his ears at this new realization. He paced between the windows to get better views. More houses. More trees. These trees were so much fuller than what he remembered. And the ground was different. *I don't see rocks, dust, or dry bushes,* he analyzed. *It's a different color too. Everything is…different!*

The truck stopped and the trailer rocked; Sir Prize adjusted his footing. His ears twitched to the left as he heard what seemed like a familiar voice. "I'll open the trailer for him," the voice said. *Could it be?*

Suddenly the trailer doors opened. And standing at the foot of the trailer was the silhouette of Missy. *Missy! Oh, I missed her!* Sir Prize nodded excitedly. She came into the trailer and kissed his forehead. He leaned into her and nodded his head up and down against her. They settled into overdue pats and hugs.

If I could hug you like a human, I'd do it. Sir Prize snorted in relief. *Reunited at last! I thought it would never happen!*

"So glad you're here," she said with a huge smile. She added a lead rope to his halter and walked him out to his new world. Chap patiently waited by the trailer, wagging his tail to greet Sir Prize. *Oh, my goodness! Chap, my pal, my friend!* Sir Prized swished his tail in unison with Chap's tail wag.

"Welcome to your new home in Missouri, my friend," Missy said.

What is a Missouri? Sir Prize jerked his ears back.

THE LOST TWIN

As Missy carefully led Sir Prize down the trailer ramp, she explained to him that she had to move all of her things to Missouri too. "I had a different trailer that I had to load and haul here, so my friend brought you for me!" she said pointing to the lady with the painted trailer. The lady came over to shake Missy's hand.

"Well, he was a mighty fine pony to haul!" she exclaimed, throwing her hands on her hips. "No trouble at all. Although I could tell he must have been missing you because he just wasn't a typical happy pony. But a lot of horses go through that in long hauls."

"Yeah, he doesn't like moves," Missy shook her head. "But he's here now. We'll be sure to get him back into the swing of things."

Missy walked Sir Prize around for a bit to stretch his legs. She finally moved him near a pasture area. His hooves touched the new ground, and he froze. He moved his head closer to the grass, inhaling the new scent. He scraped his hooves against it, leaving round indentions.

"This is grass. Fresh, green, grass," Missy chuckled. He continued sniffing it, nostrils opened wide to let in the scent. It tickled his soft nose. It suddenly reminded him of his hay. He wiggled his lips and took a bite. This was fresh, chewy, and perhaps even juicy. *This is unlike anything I've ever tasted*, Sir Prize thought as he crunched the juicy stalks.

Missy patted his shoulders. "Unfortunately, you weren't really exposed to this in your old place. But here," she waved her hand out in front of her, "there is a large pasture for your grazing leisure." Sir Prize looked up and saw a field of green in front of him. *Nothing but this fresh….grass, did you call it?* he recalled.

As Sir Prize took in his new surroundings of the new horse community, he realized it may be a little different than what he was used to back in California. The trees were so lush, this new grass so…lush. *I need a different word than "lush"*, Sir Prize shook his head.

Missy led him straight to a fence surrounding a pasture, other horses grazed off in the distance. Sir Prize had never seen such a sight! The place was surrounded by trees with large, far-reaching branches. Their canopies swayed in the breeze, as if dancing to nature's cool breath. The grass waved back to the trees, giving the illusion of a duet between the landscapes. Sir Prize broke his trance of the nature dance and noticed the horses off in the distant, all with their noses in the dancing grass. *Wait…one isn't a horse*, Sir Prize observed. Lifting his own nose for a better view, he could tell that one of the horses was significantly smaller than the others. *Another one my size? Oh, my goodness!* Sir Prize was excited for this new discovery. *I…I don't think I've ever met one before*, he realized.

"Let's get you settled into your new home first," Missy guided Sir Prize to a new barn.

So, this is my new home! Sir Prize was both relieved and terrified. He didn't want to go on any more trailer rides; but he really wanted his California home back. *Another…new…barn*, he sighed. But he was so elated to see Missy, that he just accepted his fate. And the idea of meeting another pony was a little intriguing to him.

The barn was tall and white, the outside boards showing small signs of wear and tear. Sir Prize has never met a barn that didn't look inviting. There's something about them that beckons an animal to rest there.

Generally, their big doors are like that of a grandmother's arms: open wide, welcoming, secure. As Missy led Sir Prize through those wide doors, the typical barn smells hit his nose: hay, feed, old wood, and yes, even manure.

Missy in front of the Mason barn near Queeny Park in Town and Country, MO; Sir Prize's first home in Missouri

Missy settled him into his stall and started her old routine. This calmed Sir Prize's spirit and helped him feel more at home in this new barn. But only because of Missy's presence. Everything else was too new to process or appreciate, even if pieces of it seemed no different than previous barns. As Missy brushed Sir Prize's back, a voice called out in the distance.

"Missy! Did your pony come today?" asked the voice.

"Yes! Sir Prize is here!" Missy yelled back.

The new voice belonged to another lady that Sir Prize did not recognize. As she passed Sir Prize, he realized that she was leading the pony from the pasture into the stall next to him. *The pony is my neighbor? This is wonderful!* The frustration and confusion of the move lifted in an instant. Sir Prize was excited to make a new friend!

"Sir Prize, this is Cecil," Missy explained as she finished her final brush stroke.

Cecil and Sir Prize stretched their necks out to sniff each other. Cecil's eyes were calm and welcoming. His fur was chestnut with white "socks" on his legs. Sir Prize could tell that he was much older than him, but just as warm and kind as Missy.

Welcome to the Mason barn! Cecil nodded in gesture. *I'll show you around, no worries.*

*****

Cecil and Sir Prize instantly bonded. Cecil's chill and wiser presence helped Sir Prize feel more at home when he desperately missed California. Cecil needed a friend like Sir Prize, one of his size and demeanor. They were inseparable, like lost twins who finally found each other.

Sir Prize had never experienced the mid-west summer. The summer days in Missouri were accompanied by suffocating humidity, like an irritable hot, wet blanket that covered the entire terrain. This also meant that flies — big, biting flies — used animals as food, making the horses and ponies miserable. Sir Prize never experienced this in California. No amount of Missy's presence, no amount of fresh green grass, no amount of apple snacks gave Sir Prize comfort from the humid days or armor against the biting flies.

Pure torture, this is! Why are we even here? I think I'd rather be on a trailer than be in this oven. At least I didn't get eaten alive when I was on a trailer! Oh, my goodness! What is this? He asked Cecil, twitching his muscles to agitate the flies away from him.

Cecil just chewed slowly, carefully observing Sir Prize. *You don't know about flies?* he asked curiously.

Flies? They bite? We didn't have this in California! Sir Prize twitched his ears back as a fly crawled toward his eye.

*Well, that tail of yours is supposed to help. You need to swish it more. Like this...*Cecil swished his tail all the way up over his back, a swarm of flies instantly lifted, buzzing in protest.

Wha...you just...I've never swished mine that dramatically before! Sir Prize watched in amazement at his friend.

Cecil cocked his head to the side *Well, we can stand near each other and swish them away from our faces too. Like this...*Cecil moved to where his head was next to Sir Prize's tail and Sir Prize's head was next to Cecil's tail. Cecil swished his tail and it lightly brushed against Sir Prize's nose. The irritating fly in Sir Prize's eye buzzed away.

That's brilliant! Sir Prize perked his ears forward with delight. Sir Prize swished his tail harder, his tail brushed Cecil's face in return.

Yep, just like that Cecil confirmed. For the remainder of the afternoon, they stayed close to each other grazing, but shared fly-bite interruption chores.

*****

From that day forward, Sir Prize relied on Cecil to help adjust to Missouri's both pleasant and irritating wonders. Although the summer brought nasty fly bites, the winter brought something more delicate – snow.

Sir Prize didn't mind the cooler temperatures as his fur coat automatically adjusted its length to provide warmth. But his curiosity was that of a small child as he stepped into the white, freezing flakes for the first time. He dropped his nostrils onto the snow, flaring his nostrils and taking in a whiff. The snow floated up and made a ring around his nose. He quickly lifted his head, shaking the residue off, astonished at his new wet nose.

Cecil laughed. *Let me guess, you didn't have snow in California either.*

Sir Prize, still wide-eyed from the new experience, shifted shyly in the snow. *No. This is so neat! So beautiful.* He stood looking at the terrain that was now covered in the white frosting. The world seemed more peaceful as the snow tenderly fell from the sky.

What is this? Sir Prized asked.

Well, it's too cold here for water to fall from the sky. So, it comes in various forms this time of year. This is snow, A delightful gift from the heavens. Children love this stuff! They'll play all day in it. His face turned more serious. *But we have to watch for the days when the water is more ice than snow. Those are the nasty days. We stay in the barn those days.* Cecil instructed.

Sir Prize pawed the ground and found nature's hibernating grass underneath the white carpet. It was wet from the snow's melt; not as tempting as he originally thought it would be.

Yeah, this is when those dry flakes of hay come in handy. Comfort food, he laughed. He watched his friend enjoy his new experience and longed for his younger days.

*****

Almost a full year had gone by since Sir Prize moved to Missouri. Sir Prize noticed that Cecil walked slower and stayed longer in his stall than the pasture.

Hey Cecil, you feeling ok? Sir Prize slowed to match Cecil's pace.

Yeah — just not a spring chicken anymore! Cecil said, huffing harder than earlier in the day.

Spring chicken? Well, you don't look anything like a chicken, Cecil! Sir Prize lifted his lip in laughter.

Sir Prize was always patient while he waited for his friend. He would graze near the barn, just to stay close to Cecil if he was still in his stall. Eventually, Cecil would come out when he was ready to engage in their daily routine. Any senior animal like Cecil requires a little more patience and understanding as their movements are slower.

One morning, Sir Prize grazed a little further away from the barn than usual. He ate most of the grass closest to their pasture entrance, trying to stay close to Cecil every day. However, he needed to walk a few more yards away for juicier nibbles. He didn't realize how much

Cecil, Sir Prize's best friend

time passed until he heard someone at the barn. He raised his head, refocusing his eyes on the distant scene. Cecil still wasn't out of his stall, but Missy was down there talking to Cecil's owner. The commotion around the barn seemed more urgent, their actions were a bit fast and jerky. The tone in their voices were raised. Sir Prize had not seen Missy like this before so his attention to eating suddenly vanished. Another human appeared and all three went into Cecil's stall. *What is going on?* Sir Prize widened his nostrils, lifting his head higher.

After a few moments of not seeing additional movement, Sir Prize slowly moved his head to the grass. Just as he was about to take a bite, he heard the humans. "Ok, almost there," Missy's voice echoed across the pasture. Sir Prize shot his head back up, twitched his ears toward the barn to listen better. Missy walked backwards out of Cecil's stall, holding a corner of a large tarp and Cecil's nose peaked out of it. Immediately the rest of the crew followed, all holding the tarp that carried Cecil's weight. Sir Prize's mane shivered as he realized what happened. His heart felt like a brick in his chest. He started to walk faster toward the barn. Although the humans covered Cecil as much as they could, Sir Prize still got a closer glimpse of his lifeless nostril and lips. Sir Prize eagerly walked into his stall. He no longer wanted pasture time. He immediately wanted California. He needed comfort.

Missy went into his stall. She knew that this was the first time Sir Prize witnessed the death of a dear friend. And not just any friend, his best friend. She slowly brushed him. No words…just the sound of the brush against his back. Sir Prize faced the corner away from the window, head hung low in grief and despair. For hours, Missy and Chap stayed with him. They all grieved as the sun surrendered to the moon.

THE DRILL SERGEANT

For days, Sir Prize grieved, not leaving his stall. Visitors would stop by, offering treats or fresh vegetables, but he didn't want to be social. Missy explained to them that since Cecil's passing, he was in mourning and his appetite wasn't the same. The visitors would leave their snacks and Missy would add it to his feed for eating when he was ready. She'd stay a little longer in the mornings and afternoons, brushing him just as she had on that day. Even though he didn't need grooming, it was Missy's way of comforting him, letting him know that he wasn't alone.

Cecil's stall was still open, a reminder of his missed presence. It had been cleaned and stripped of anything that Cecil used, now just a bare shell of wooden walls. Sir Prize dreaded the day he had a new neighbor. He wasn't ready to make new friends.

After a few weeks, Sir Prize finally ventured back to the pasture, but only because Missy made him go. He started to feel a bit better with the fresh air, sun, and juicy grass to chew. As he lost himself in the moments of grazing, he heard a familiar creaking. A trailer.

No! Sir Prize huffed. *Not now! I'm not going!*

As he watched the trailer in the distance, he realized it wasn't Missy this time. As a matter of fact, a new, spotted pony stepped out of it. Sir Prize curiously watched the pony and his owner from the pasture, intrigued by the new addition to the horse community. Then the human directed the new pony into Cecil's old stall. Sir Prize's ears immediately jerked backward. *Well, I guess I have a new neighbor.*

Later that evening Missy brought Sir Prize over to meet the new tenant. But the new pony had no interest in meeting Sir Prize. He kept his back turned toward the stall door. *That's fine.* Sir Prize thought. *I don't really want to get to know you right now anyways.*

"Sir Prize, this is Cochise," Missy mentioned as she gave him hay. "He pulls a cart! Someday, we're doing that too!"

What is this "cart" thing you're talking about? Sir Prize's imagination ran with images of a wheelbarrow strapped to his back. That's the only cart he ever saw. *How would that even work?*

*****

As days turned into weeks, Cochise still didn't interact with any other horses or Sir Prize. His interactions were mostly with the humans around him. Sir Prize was irritated because Cochise's attitude was down-right rude! No "hellos", no "how are you"s…just complete disregard for any of his equine brothers and sisters. Cochise acted like he was the only pony in the whole Mason barn. And although Sir Prize was still grieving, he missed having another pony friend.

Sir Prize would watch Cochise as his owner gave riding lessons to various students. His demeanor wasn't pleasant. Often, he made it difficult for new riders, resulting in very few young riders taking lessons with him. It was as if Cochise deliberately tested the riders to stay on his back. His head would be high, daring the riders to yank on the reins the wrong way just once so he could spin in resistance. Cochise eyes were gleaming with attitude, *not my problem if you can't handle me, kid.* Sir Prize hadn't seen this much feistiness in a horse or pony in years – perhaps ever.

Cochise's interest in making friends at the barn was as absent as Cecil's gentle presence. He was all business and stern, as if he should have been part of the military calvary. Sir Prize considered him like a drill sergeant. Cochise pushed the riders' will to ride, dared the rider to make the wrong move, and challenged the rider to earn his respect.

Cochise would act completely different around his owner, surrendering to her commands. On occasion, his owner would strap him to a device with a bench hoisted above two wheels. *Is this the cart Missy mentioned?* Sir Prize pondered. After a few more tugs on the straps, his owner would climb onto the bench, snap the reins, and off Cochise trotted, dragging the cart behind him like a respectable and compliant pony.

Cochise, the "drill sergeant"

*****

After a few months passed, Sir Prize got used to Cochise rude yet quiet ways. The ponies never exchanged pleasantries or friendly glances. However, Missy and Cochise's human seemed to have sparked a friendship. They would pair up and lead trail ride lessons for students. Missy always told her students that being a rider was not just about learning to ride but about teaching others to respect horses, ponies, and the sport. "When you are with the horse, you are an ambassador for the horse. The horse cannot speak human languages. You must speak for them." As always, Sir Prize took pride in Missy being his "human". He loved how she taught others to respect animals.

One day, Missy assembled a group of experienced riders together for a trail ride. Missy instructed, "Today, we are going to ride to Queeny Park's event called 'Animal Planet Pet Day'. Here, you will be expected to play the ambassador on behalf of your horse. You are responsible for informing others about horses, riding, and answer whatever questions they may have."

And with those instructions, Missy led the trail riders toward the event. Sir Prize, Cochise, and other horses all had one of their regular students at the reins. The group fell into a comfortable assembly and trail pace. The trail led to a clearing which hosted hundreds of people, various animals of all sizes (although mostly smaller than the horses and ponies on the trail), and several yards away a giant hot air balloon. Sir Prize gaped at the sights in front of him, ears twitching in various directions.

The riders formed a line with their horses and ponies, side-by-side, providing a majestic display of disciplined riders. The beauty of the formation caught the eyes of the event attendees. Several excited people approached the group, asking questions.

"Whoa! This is so cool! Horses!" said one child.

"Can I pet the horse?" asked another.

"Can I ride?" asked another.

"How big is he?" asked a taller man.

"Can I take a picture?" asked a woman.

As the people started to come closer to the horses and ponies, the riders remained calm and answered all the questions they could. Sir

Prize watched Cochise from the side, expecting him to act out in his rebellious way considering this was new for all of them. But he stood proud. Almost as if for every person that came by, he was saying *Thank you ma'am* or *Thank you sir*, giving the indication he wasn't this defiant horse that would buck you in a heartbeat. Sir Prize imagined him with a drill sergeant hat as he acted stoic around the strangers.

Suddenly the whoosh of the fire in the hot air balloon broke the questioning and interest. It startled several horses. Thankfully, the riders remained calm, and the horses remained in place. Again, the whoosh bombed the air waves as the balloon filled with hot air. The people said their goodbyes to the riders as they moved to the balloon activities.

Missy directed the riders to head back to the barn. The horses and ponies had enough excitement for the day. They slowly retraced the trail back from which they came. The riders chattered and laughed about the other animals they saw.

Sir Prize enjoyed the happy human conversations but eventually his attention narrowed again to Cochise. Cochise was directly in front of him. His body swayed confidently, no hesitation in his gate, no fatigue as his head held high. *I'm constantly intrigued by him* Sir Prize thought. *He demands respect. He earns respect. But in unconventional ways. He's always "on", ready for the next challenge. Nothing phases him.*

Back at the barn, the riders started their routine of removing saddles, bridles, and brushing down their equine friends. All horses and ponies were fed, watered, and loved on before the riders left. The barn noise faded into distant crickets chirping, the sun a fading sliver of orange. As Sir Prize finished his hay, his thoughts wondered through the day's events, and then back to Cochise. *His behaviors are so dynamic. With new riders he is all over the place. With experienced riders that stick with him, he is proud. With his human, he is compliant and soft.* Sir Prize agrees with his comparison of a drill sergeant, but ultimately Cochise is a fierce trainer of riders. His tactics challenged riders to overcome their fears and apprehension. *Although, I prefer the nicer approach where they love me and I get snacks,* Sir Prize humored himself.

EXPERIENCED RIDER WANTED

Sir Prize, Cochise and the other horses were lazily grazing in the pasture when Sir Prize noticed Missy around the barn, Chap close to her side. He then spotted a couple of girls walking toward Missy, their body language was friendly with smiles and nods. Finally, one of the girls pointed to the pasture. He watched as Missy and the girl walked in his direction. Sir Prize recognized the girl as a regular rider of Cochise. Just as Missy reached Sir Prize, the girl started to lead Cochise out of the pasture; he followed her without issues. Missy slipped a halter onto Sir Prize's face, feeding him his treats as usual as she led him back to the barn.

Missy went into trainer mode, talking to the girl who was with Cochise. "So, your sister will be riding my pony, Sir Prize. He does very well with new riders, but as you know, you'll need to be aware of the surroundings and how the animals react to it," Missy instructed.

"Don't worry, Missy! I'll help out," said Cochise's rider.

Sir Prize wasn't too worried about a new rider, that's his job. And he wasn't worried about trail riding, he was used to that too. The difference was that this rider wasn't trained with Sir Prize. And he didn't know if this rider had any riding experience. Sometimes, there were creeks and holes that Sir Prize must maneuver around or jump over for better footing. A rider should know how to move appropriately as a horse or pony balanced on the terrain.

The sisters proceeded to guide the ponies to the trailhead, Cochise and his experienced rider leading the way. He was always a little faster, causing a gap between him and any horse behind him. Or in this, case, Sir Prize. *Figures,* Sir Prize grunted.

Sir Prize could tell immediately that his rider wasn't trained. She held the reins too tight and sat stiff in the saddle. Usually when Missy trained riders, they do not trail ride until they learned basic riding skills in the corral. After the basic lessons, then Missy would walk with them on the trail to provide clear instructions on how the rider should anticipate the horse's or pony's movements. It was a more controlled environment for both the rider and equine partner to learn to trust each other.

But this is my job, to keep her safe. Sir Prize thought. So even though the rider didn't move with him as she should, he took ownership of the ride. As they continued and his concentration deepened, the gap between him and Cochise widened. *I hate following Cochise; I'm always behind. And with the new rider, I'm being extra cautious.* Sir Prize continued down the trail, slowly walking over rocks, roots, and other known crevasses. *So far so good,* he assessed.

They neared a creek that Sir Prize knew very well, but this required a small jump across one section. Sir Prize readied himself for the quick jump, same as always. *The rider isn't adjusting as I'm expecting,* Sir Prize observed. *They need to stand a bit in the stirrups.* The rider still sat in the saddle. Looking ahead, Cochise already completed the jump. *Maybe that will be the cue for the rider, perhaps she saw the other rider move.* Still, the rider remained seated.

Sir Prize realized he had to make the jump without the rider adjusting. Unfortunately, in this part of the path, there weren't other choices but to make the jump. It's a small one. Any horse or pony can do it in their sleep, but with a rider, the balancing act can be tricky. Sir Prize steadied his gait, then leaped just enough to make the jump. Just as he landed on the other side, his left back hoof didn't grab the ground as it normally did. In that split second, he felt a pop in his leg. Pain instantly flushed through his leg and made him stumble. *But the rider!* Sir Prize instantly caught himself with his other legs...but barely.

"Whoa buddy," the rider said.

"Everything ok?" Cochise's rider asked, turning Cochise around.

"I don't know. He stumbled," said Sir Prize's rider.

Sir Prize kept going, determined to not disappoint the rider or give Cochise an excuse to disrespect him more. *I'm fine, let's keep going,* Sir Prize stubbornly thought.

"Well, he seems fine," said the other rider. "Let's keep moving." And with that, she turned Cochise back around to keep heading down the trail. Cochise gave Sir Prize a disapproving look right before he swayed his head to the front, accenting his disappointment with a swift swish of his tail.

As they rode, Sir Prize gingerly used his back left leg. He couldn't put much weight on it. He kept thinking *I just need to keep the rider safe.* He never lost a student thanks to Missy's training. *And I won't start today.*

By the time they approached the end of the trail, Sir Prize was in agony. He tired quickly from balancing on three legs and limping with the fourth. But the riders didn't notice. They continued with their laughter and chatter, oblivious to the injured pony.

Suddenly Missy rushed to them, waving her arms and yelling "Get off! Get off him now!"

The riders exchanged confused glances.

"Can't you see he is limping? Get off! Now!" Missy commanded to Sir Prize's rider.

Both riders immediately dismounted. As soon as Sir Prize felt the weight of his rider off his back, Sir Prize was able to relax. He finally broke his concentration on the rider and now the body wanted its turn of his attention, pain radiated all over his back leg.

"When a horse is limping, you immediately get off. Immediately!" Missy said with a stern voice, eyes glaring with anger at the riders.

"I – I didn't really notice. He stumbled a little after he jumped at the creek," Sir Prize's rider's voice trembled with fear.

"And you didn't think to check what was wrong?" Missy asked.

"He seemed fine after that," the rider insisted. "I'm so sorry. I didn't know."

Missy sighed and closed her eyes. After a few brief moments she responded, "I know. We need to get him in his stall right away." Her voice was strained but remained calm.

They all walked to the stalls together; Missy stayed with Sir Prize's pace. The riders took care of Cochise, removing his saddle and preparing his stall.

Missy whispered in Sir Prize's ear. "Oh, my poor boy! We need to get your leg looked at immediately." Her voice was shaking, perhaps even crying. *Missy, it's ok. I did my job. The rider didn't fall off like you trained me,* Sir Prize thought. He nuzzled his nose next to her side, hoping to make her feel better. He continued to stumble as they made their way to the barn. *It's been a long time since I wanted to be in my stall and away from people. I'm feeling that now.* His eyes were heavy from pain and exhaustion.

Missy fed him his food, hay, and water. Sir Prize barely grazed; the he was too distracted from the pain. He couldn't put his left back leg down without grunting or stumbling. Missy carefully wrapped it with an ice pack; as soon as the ice melted, she'd repack it with fresh ice and re-apply. This routine went on for hours. Sometimes Sir Prize would hear Missy muttering softly. "I can't believe…", "why would they….", "if only I…". Sir Prize couldn't make out the rest of the sentences. He was too distracted from the pain to understand.

*****

"He has a bowed tendon," said the vet.

"His jumping days are over. They're over!" Missy sighed heavily, placing her hands on her hips.

"Probably. But, with the right care, he can be back on all fours and at a minimum doing small activities, such as walking," assured the vet.

Missy shook her head. "I think I'm more frustrated at myself than anything. I didn't train that rider and I didn't know that rider, so I couldn't assure Sir Prize's safety. I just took for granted that the other rider *was* experienced and should have given her sister pointers. Ugh!" Missy shook her head in frustration and ran her hand down her face.

Sir Prize listened intently. Missy's voice over the last couple of days was very gentle with him but when she talked to other people, her voice was more agitated.

"Well, you know the routine. Use cold-hosing and ice wraps. Keep him quiet and total stall rest. Give him and yourself time. Do not rush the treatments," explained the vet, dusting off his dirty hands. He patted Sir Prize gently on his shoulder, indicating he was done with his examination.

"Yes sir! I've been around horses and ponies long enough to know the drill. It's just a shame that this happened," Missy continued to shake her head.

Every day, Missy doctored Sir Prize. She ran cold water down his leg for twenty minutes at a time, several times a day. Between the cold-hosing, she wrapped his leg with ice packs. After each session, Sir Prize's leg felt a little better. As days passed, he no longer felt the sharp pain he did in those initial days of the injury.

After several weeks of treatments, Missy put a halter on his head. "Alright boy, let's see if we can walk you from the stall to that fence a few yards away," instructed Missy, her voice seemed to be a little more positive today.

Sir Prize took a few steps, his left back leg still a little shaky. *Hey! I can use it a bit more now!* Sir Prize thought. But after several steps, he started to limp again. *Oh shoot! I guess not.* Sir Prize suddenly felt discouraged.

"Ok boy, that's all for today. I just wanted to see how far we can go," Missy said. Her facial expression was still hopeful but seemed to be calculating how many steps he took before he started to limp again. "We'll try again in a few days."

Missy completed the therapy routine every day for a couple of months. Sir Prize was used to the new routine. Every day he gained more strength, but still his injury lingered. *Will I ever be completely healed?* Sir Prize wondered.

One day, after Missy completed a treatment session, she gathered his buckets, his halters, and his treats. *What? What are you doing?* Sir Prize thought. Then he heard it. A trailer.

Sir Prize grunted, *not again!*

THE MENDING MEADOW

The trailer ride was the shortest ride Sir Prize ever experienced. Although Sir Prize didn't understand time or distance, he calculated that it took him longer to eat his breakfast than it did to move him to this new place. It was a quaint, cozy barn, with Sir Prize as the only tenant. And honestly, Sir Prize was ok with some alone time. His social mood had changed after losing his best friend, living next to the "drill sergeant", and suffering his injury. He was ready for some relaxation. *Wonder if I'll get bored though,* Sir Prize thought. *I may miss the actions of a horse barn community.* But he quickly shrugged that away. In his older years, social engagement wasn't as exciting as it used to be.

As Missy prepped his stall and Chap chased squirrels, he studied his surroundings. It was like out of a fantasy story book. To his left was Missy's new house, sitting on top of the hill several yards away from the barn. The steep hill towered over the barn, covered in bushes and small shrubs. Human or animal footsteps created a small dirt path from the barn to the house. Sir Prize assumed this was Missy's route to the barn. From the looks of that hill, even a four-legged creature like Sir Prize would have to be careful walking up or down it because it was so steep. To his right, was an open, flat meadow. Sir Prize figured no one could see this meadow very well from the quiet, neighborhood road at the top of the hill. The meadow was in the middle of a large, wooded valley that contained thick grass, flowers, and a shallow, rocky creek. Everything about this meadow seemed like something out of a princess fairy tale. *This place is amazing!* Sir Prize thought, stunned by its beauty. In front of him, the barn was small, cozy, and welcoming. It had two main horse stalls, a large storage room, and a garage area with doors that opened

The barn in the meadow, corral fenced removed

to the wide meadow pasture. The sun faded the red paint over the years, leaving the impression of horse stories from the past. A small corral extended out into the yard, forming an area for Sir Prize to roam next to the barn.

Off in the distance a herd of deer strolled through the woods, stopping to pick up fallen acorns and nuts from the trees. The sun glowed through the trees on the hill, draping the valley with strips of warm light. The air was fresh and clean. Sir Prize's nostrils flared to breathe in the different smells of the meadow, perked his ears at the sounds of birds. So many new sounds, new smells, and new sights filled his senses. And it was all his, *and mine alone,* he thanked.

The meadow and barn yard were at the end of a large strip of backyards of nearby homes. The flat valley exposed the view of playsets and outside toys. *Children!* Sir Prize thought, with a glimmer of hope.

A few days later, children from next door stopped by the barn while Missy cleaned Sir Prize's stall.

"Can we pet him?" they asked in their tiny voices.

"Of course!" Missy said.

"We have carrots," they said, holding up a bunch of whole carrots in their small hands. "Can we feed them to him?"

"Oh, he loves carrots! He'll be so happy." Missy helped the two children share the carrots with Sir Prize. They petted his soft nose and asked a lot of questions.

"What's his name? How old is he? What's his favorite food?" they rambled on as Sir Prize listened. Missy patiently answered all the questions. *Again, always the teacher,* Sir Prize admired.

"Can we ride him?" they asked.

Missy chuckled. "Unfortunately, not right now. You see his back leg," she asked, pointing to his injured leg. "It is in pretty bad shape from an accident a couple of months ago. He's still healing. But, if he gets better, then we can talk," Missy said with a wink.

"Awww," whined the kids. "We're so sorry, Sir Prize!" They patted his nose, feeling sorry for the pony. *Well, aren't you kids sweet?* Sir Prize amused.

After a few more moments of questions, their mom waved them back over to their backyard. "Ok we have to go. Bye, Sir Prize," they said, walking away and waving their tiny hands.

*****

As time passed, Sir Prize got used to his new home in the quiet meadow. Missy continued her therapy sessions on Sir Prize's leg; however, he could walk longer distances without much of a limp. The vet came back to check on him.

"I see you're in a new place!" he said, surveying the meadow.

"Yeah, we moved here to this meadow and small barn so that Sir Prize could have some peace and quiet while healing. The other barn was too busy and I always worried that someone would accidently make it worse by letting him out to the pasture or by walking into his stall without knowing his injury," Missy explained.

"This is a nice area! Just perfect for a pony like him," the vet said while running his hand down Sir Prize's leg.

My leg is doing much better, doc! Sir Prize thought. He turned his head to the vet, just seeing his back. Sir Prize nuzzled his lips over his jacket, smelling other scents he didn't recognize.

The vet chuckled at Sir Prize's welcoming gesture. "Well, you're in a good mood!" He patted Sir Prize's forehead and scratched between his ears. Sir Prize lifted his head for a deeper scratch. *Ahhh yes, right there!*

"Well, looks like you did all the right things. If anything, he seems to be stronger than expected! I'll leave it up to you on what activities you start but he should be good to go. He's all clear in my book!" said the vet, again dusting off his hands just as he did with his first visit.

*****

One afternoon, Sir Prize leaned against the corral fence, enjoying the sun's warmth on his back. Half asleep, he barely noticed the new human near the barn door.

"Missy?" the stranger called out. He extended his hand into the corral at Sir Prize, apple slices in his hand.

Sir Prize's eyes snapped awake. *Oh, I like you already,* Sir Prize thought, accepting the delicious gift.

"Hey Terry!" said Missy, as she walked out to greet him.

"You all settled in ok?" Terry asked Missy.

"Yep! We really appreciate you letting us rent this place from you. It is absolutely perfect for us!" Missy gushed.

"Well of course! What are friends for?" Terry chuckled, giving Missy a hug.

"Although, I have some questions about the barn if you have a minute," Missy said as she wiped the sweat from her forehead.

"Sure thing!" and just like that, Terry and Missy disappeared into the barn, leaving Sir Prize to his sunbathing.

After that day, Terry would visit from time-to-time, often fixing items at the barn as Missy requested. Sir Prize would hear loud noises coming from the barn – a thud, a whack, a ping. Each noise triggered Sir Prize to shift his ears. Several minutes after the noises, Terry would come out, dust off his hands, and say "Well, that's fixed." Every time he stopped by the barn, he treated Sir Prize to various snacks. Sometimes Missy was there when he visited, sometimes she wasn't. Either way, Terry became a regular visitor for Sir Prize and a regular mender of the barn.

Terry's visits often brought some excitement to Sir Prize's day. Considering Sir Prize no longer lived in a horse community, he looked forward to any human visit. As soon as Sir Prize saw him coming down the hill, he'd quickly walk over to the corral fence, anxiously awaiting the goodness Terry had in his hand.

One late summer day, Terry made his way to the corral. The air was hot and dry, almost like California days. Grateful for the distraction, Sir Prize walked to the corral fence. He pushed his nose through the bars.

"Hey buddy," Terry greeted, petting his nose.

Hey buddy, Sir Prize thought, wiggling his nose for any familiar scent of snacks. *What do you have for me today? Apples? Carrots? Oh, I can't wait!*

He sniffed the man's fingers but no treat. With a snarky tone in his head, Sir Prize nuzzled his lips into his palm. *Treats for petting. That's the deal,* Sir Prize humored himself.

After a few scratches on the head, Terry rolled a small, ripe watermelon under the bottom bar of the corral. "Here you go buddy! I figured you might like this!"

Sir Prize twitched his ears back. *What is THAT?* He walked over and sniffed it. *It smells edible.* He moved his lips over it to bite it, but he couldn't grab it with his teeth. *What? How?* Sir Prize was very confused by this new food. As he attempted to bite it and grab it with his lips, it would roll away.

"Have fun with that, buddy! I gotta run." Terry tapped the corral bar twice, a cue that he was leaving. Sir Prize barely heard him as he was in deep concentration on how to eat this new treat. *How do I bite this thing? My lips can't get a grip! It's too big. Too slippery.*

A few hours went by as Sir Prize nibbled at it, nosed it, pawed at it, anything to try to eat it. It entertained him so much that little did he realize he pushed it close to the corral fence. With one big push of his hoof, the watermelon rolled back under the corral fence, just out of reach for him. He tried to put his head through the fence, but his head was too big. *Ugh, now what?* He stared at it for a while but finally gave up, walking into his stall for some water. *That was quite the workout!*

That evening, Missy came down to the barn as usual to complete the feeding routine. As she walked into corral, she noticed the watermelon out of the corner of her eye. She literally stopped in her tracks and just stared at it for a moment.

Hey, can you get that back in here for me? Sir Prize pleaded, vigorously nodding his head up and down.

Curious, she called her friend. "Terry, hey how's it going," Missy asked casually. "You mentioned you were going to stop by today. Did you happen to bring a watermelon with you?"

Sir Prize shifted his position as Missy pushed his rear so she could get to his feed bucket. He listened intently. *"Watermelon"? That's new!*

"So, you just rolled the whole thing into the corral?" Missy laughed, one hand on the metal device by her ear, the other taking a brush to his back. "Oh, that's funny!" She paused. "I recommend next time breaking it up for Sir Prize. Horse lips and teeth don't work well enough to break an object that large or one with that thick of a rind."

Missy went on to tell him that Sir Prize managed to roll it back under the corral and outside of reach.

"Oh, I wish I had a camera setup to watch that fun activity!" Missy said out loud. She said her goodbyes to the metal device and shoved it back in her pocket. She continued to chuckle as she took out her pocketknife, cutting up the watermelon for Sir Prize. "Here you go, buddy. What do you think of this?"

Sir Prize quivered his lips over the now-exposed, juicy insides of the melon. *Oh, sweet heavens! This is amazing!* He quickly ate all the watermelon. *This was so worth the wait!*

HOLIDAY SHENANIGANS

Summer turned into fall; leaves changed into vibrant colors. Sir Prize waded through the thick ocean of leaves in the meadow, pushing them out of the way for one clump of juicy grass at a time. Sir Prize got used to the smells of wood burning in near-by firepits or chimneys. The air was cooler and pleasing to his furred skin.

One crisp fall day, the mother from next-door came by to talk to Missy. "Hi, Missy! How are you?" she asked as she approached the stall. She and Missy started to chit chat about the kids, weather, and other things that Sir Prize just tuned out as he ate his feed.

"Hey, I was wondering if I could ask a favor. My son wants to be a knight for Halloween and he would love it if you'd be willing to bring Sir Prize along, even if it is just for pictures," asked the mother.

"That would be so fun!" Missy said to the mom. "I think that sounds like a great idea."

Overhearing this, Sir Prize shook his head. *Sometimes I don't want to be people's amusement. Sometimes I just want to be left alone to graze on the grass. Sometimes I just want to be doing my thing.* Sir Prize wished again he could speak human to say it in a mocking tone like it was in his head.

After a few weeks, Sir Prize forgot about that little conversation. The days were the same routine of feeding, meadow grazing, and children visiting. On the evening of Halloween, Missy came down to the barn to get Sir Prize ready for the requested adventure. The routine started out normal. Yet, Sir Prize knew something was different when she started the saddling routine. The last time Sir Prize was out this late was one of his old training days at the Mason barn. He wasn't in the mood to do extra work. Usually by now he was in his stall, ready to chill for the night.

Missy led Sir Prize up the steep hill and instead of turning right to walk down the street like they often do on their walks, she turned left and went straight into the neighbor's front yard. *Odd,* Sir Prize noted. As they waited, Missy loosened the lead rope so Sir Prize could graze on the grass. Just as Sir Prize lowered his head to the grass, there were a collision of voices coming from the front door of the house. Sir Prize twitched his ears back in protest.

"Don't run up to him! You need to wait!" yelled the mother as a little kid came running out of the house.

What is he wearing? Sir Prize tipped his head to the side to get a better look.

The little boy hobbled toward Sir Prize, clanking with his plastic knight armor. "I'm a knight and you are my trusty horse!" he said, the helmet clearly oversized for his head. He waved a short plastic sword toward Sir Prize.

Sir Prize recognized the voice as one of the little kids who gives him carrots. As the boy hobbled toward them, Missy walked over to help him. He seemed a little uncoordinated in all the gear he wore. The mother was distracted, corralling the other child who was not interested in the brother's plan of events.

What do I know about being part of a knight's defense system? Nothing! Sir Prize was annoyed at being there. He decided *nope* and just flopped down on the grass, grunted dramatically as he rolled to his resting spot, stretching his legs out for better comfort. He strained his neck out smelling the wonderful grass. *Hmmm, they have good grass here,* Sir Prize noted.

The mother shrieked in horror. "Oh my god, is he ok? Do we need to call a vet?"

Missy shook her head, sighing. "No, this is his version of a three-year-old's tantrum. He is trying to tell us he doesn't want to do this." Missy said while rolling her eyes.

"My horse is dead!" cried the little knight. Wailing continued which scared the other child, who also started to cry. The mother did her best to console both children, but it was a losing battle.

"I'm so sorry," Missy said to the mother. "Do you have any apples or carrots?" she asked over the crying kids.

It was mayhem! And Sir Prize didn't care. He was tuning it all out because he was determined to eat whatever that sweet, smell was ahead of him. And if he stretched his neck and lips just enough, he would succeed in his plan of doing what he wanted (eating) and not what they wanted (playing pretend).

A few minutes passed and Sir Prize managed to tune everyone out of his mind. As he laid on his side, he lazily nibbled grass from the side of his mouth. He got his way…at least for the moment. *Wait! What is that smell? I know that smell!* Sir Prize sniffed the air instead of the grass, just barely lifting his nose from the tips of the grass blades. *Apples!* And the real apples, not the apple snacks he loved so much. His attention instantly switched to the juicy delicacy.

Missy stood in front of him but just far enough away that he couldn't reach it without standing. She had this knowing grin on her face. Sure

71

enough, Sir Prize lifted himself to stand on all four legs. Everyone cheered but he didn't care because he just got an apple which is way better than any clump of grass. *Fine. I'll be your steed for the night.*

*****

As the autumn days turned cooler and the trees were barren of their leafy coats, frost kissed the grass every morning. Sir Prize's coat grew thicker with the more consistent cold days. And although Sir Prize didn't have a calendar, the different colored lights in the distant back yards informed him that this was a special time of year.

At Christmas the meadow wore a new sparkling dress of white and the trees were trimmed with white ribbon. Sir Prize didn't have snow in his California days, so it was a new experience for him. Sir Prize saw the children next door gather it in their hands, pat it down, and then throw it at each other. They would giggle as the snow broke into smaller pieces after it hit them. Their laughter was infectious; Sir Prize started to laugh as well, making snorting noises. On occasion, they'd lie on their back, spread out their arms and legs in sweeping motion. *Rolling in snow? Oh, I can do that!*

He immediately flopped onto the snow, scattering white flakes into in the air. He rolled onto his back and punched the air with his hooves. With the right motion, his back wiggled like a worm against the cold snow. The fresh snow dampened his back, making it shiver in the cool air. The shivering excited him; he wiggled more, then faster. He popped back up on his hooves and pranced around in glee. He found a fresh spot of snow and flopped on it. As he wiggled and moved, he made his own pony-version of a snow angel. In the distance he saw the kids staring at him and laughing. Their laughs gave him renewed energy and he repeated his routine over and over.

Suddenly, he realized their giggles were absent. He looked over and they were gone. He breathed hard from his playful antics. *Perhaps I need a rest. And water,* as thirst gripped his dry mouth. As he started back to his stall, he heard a crinkle. His ears twitched; his nostrils flared. *Oh, I know that sound!* The snow hushed the meadow, amplifying any sound - including the mysterious crinkling. *And that crinkling means one thing…candy!* he nodded, heading faster toward the sound.

Sir Prize and Missy at the meadow barn during snow fall

He heard the crinkling again; his ear twitched to the left. *Yep, it's coming from that direction.* He shifted his direction to the children's house, only a few yards ahead at this point after all his excitement from earlier. As he walked closer, he heard more crinkling, louder this time. *They must have a lot of candy.* He quickly strolled to their back door. *Is this a stall door?* He couldn't get in, but he could see the family. They comfortably sat around the room, laughing as the children played around a decorated tree. The children's giggles were loud in the background as an older human popped candy into his mouth; he balled the crinkling wrapper in his hand.

The children saw Sir Prize at their back door. Not realizing it was him, they children shrieked. "Mommy! Santa brought us a pony for Christmas!" said the little girl, jumping up and down in her fuzzy slippers.

"What?" said the mother as she turned to see Sir Prize standing there. "Umm, no honey. That's Sir Prize. The pony next door! I'm not sure why he is here. I need to call Missy."

The older human unwrapped candy again, crinkling the wrapper in his hands. Sir Prize twitched his ears and nodded his head up and down hoping to use it as a clue for the humans to give him some candy. This made the children squeal with laughter. This was one of the few times in his life he wished he could speak in human words. *Oh, how I want some candy!* Sir Prize lifted his nose in the air for a better smell, lifting his lips and showing his teeth. Again, the children snickered at Sir Prize's animated face. Sir Prize concentrated so much to the candy wrapper sound he failed to see Missy approach him.

"Hey you," said Missy. "Why on earth are you over here?" She had the halter with her, but she also had some apples in her hand. She turned to the neighbors to talk and then she heard it. She heard the crinkle.

"Oh! *That* is why Sir Prize came over," she said to the neighbors. "Sir Prize must have heard the candy wrapper crinkling through your screen door. He knows that noise and it usually means peppermints. He absolutely loves that stuff!"

"Oh my!" said the neighbor. "We opened the back door just a bit to get some fresh air in while we celebrated. Sometimes if there is a fire going while there is a bunch of people in the room, it gets a little warm. That is so funny that he heard that from the meadow! Here, take some candy with you. Merry Christmas, Sir Prize!"

Missy took Sir Prize home and fed him the candy. "Merry Christmas, my friend," she said. Chap curled up next to Sir Prize, enjoying the cozy stall.

THE CART GAMES

Although December's cooler, snowy weather encouraged playful moments, January and February weather tested Sir Prize's thick, fur coat. They brought bone-chilling air and sometimes layered everything with ice and sleet. Sir Prize spent many days in the barn as he waited for warmer weather. *Yes, I like the seasons, but some can sure be on the extreme side.* he impatiently complained.

As winter gave way to milder temperatures, Sir Prize enjoyed longer days in the meadow. The transition of wintery nights into early spring days opened the first flowers of the new season. Tiny white flowers and wild, randomly placed yellow daffodils dotted the meadow with new vibrant colors. Trees budded with hints of new shade for the upcoming summer. Sir Prize was completely content in his meadow, nibbling the new green grass from the ground.

Off in the distance, Missy worked in the barn as she often did as he grazed. On occasion Sir Prize heard the typical rush of water into his bucket and the scratching of the pitchfork along the barn floor as she cleaned his stall. The familiar noises faded but Missy stayed hidden in the barn. She then appeared and walked toward Sir Prize with some objects in her hand. Sir Prize paid no attention as they didn't seem out of the ordinary.

"Hey buddy! How about some new training today?" Missy asked. She had a bridle and what appeared to be long reins in her hands. Not knowing what to expect but not alarmed yet either, Sir Prize obliged his friend. He accepted the bit into his mouth as she slipped the bridle over his head.

She then walked behind him, dragging the long reins. Sir Prize turned his head toward her. *What are you doing back there?* he thought. *What is all this about?*

She gently took up contact on the reins so she could feel if his mouth was relaxed or if he had his jaw clenched. Bits and reins were not foreign to Sir Prize; he knew what to do. He could feel what she was doing with the reins through the sensations of the bit.

Um, ok? Sir Prize questioned. *So, you're going to walk behind me with those reins.* Although he thought it was odd, he also trusted Missy. She commanded "walk on". He twitched his ears, thinking *whatever* and strolled forward. Missy was still behind him. On occasion, she'd pull the right rein. Sir Prize would turn right, like in his riding lessons. She then pulled the left rein. He'd turn left. This went on for several minutes until finally Missy gave the classic "whoa" command.

"Ok buddy, not too bad," she said. She unsnapped the reins from his bit and walked away from Sir Prize.

So odd. Sir Prize thought. *What was the point of all that?* He watched for her at the barn. He still wore the bridle as a reminder that they weren't done with whatever crazy thing Missy had planned for the day.

She walked back to Sir Prize carrying the reins, more straps, and some sort of round contraption. The straps were new but again, not alarming. Missy moved around him, adding the straps and adjusting buckles. She then attached the round contraption to the straps that draped to the ground, a few feet behind Sir Prize. *Seriously, what is this?* Sir Prize thought, ears continuing to twitch back in confusion.

"Ok buddy, now we're going to have you pull a tire," Missy said, sighing in an ambitious tone.

A "tire"? So that's what that is. And why again are we doing this? Sir Prize wished at that moment he could speak human language to let Missy know she was acting bizarre.

She again gently took up contact with the reins, Sir Prize moved but this time, he was aware of a new weight pushing on his chest. He was accustomed to weight being on top of him. The weight wasn't horrible, but it was different. Every time he tried to step forward, he felt the weight pushing against his chest, holding him back. *This is weird! I can't move forward like this!*

"Come on boy," Missy urged. "Walk through it."

Walk through it? I can't even see what I'm walking through! Sir Prize argued.

"Come on, all you have to do is walk," Missy encouraged again.

Frustrated, Sir Prize tried again. First one hoof forward. The weight pushed against his chest again. *Ok, I can feel this push against me but there's nothing in front of me preventing me to continue.* As he analyzed his situation, he moved his second leg forward. The weight sensation was still on his chest but unchanging. He stepped forward again. *Hey, ok! I get it.*

"There you go! Now you got it!" Missy praised him. As Sir Prize continued to push forward, he felt the straps around his back and side wiggle as he dragged the tire behind him.

Chap ran around them in excitement, also confused by Missy's "brilliant" agenda. *Yeah, I don't get it either,* Sir Prize agreed.

After several minutes of pulling the tire, Missy directed Sir Prize back toward the barn. She stopped him with another "whoa" then gently laid the reins down. She disappeared into the barn, just leaving Sir Prize all strapped up to this tire.

What now? Sir Prize pondered, eyes astutely studying the door.

Missy reappeared, this time with some plastic bags. The crinkling of these bags was not the same as the crinkling of the candy wrappers. Sir Prize didn't appreciate this new addition. *First random straps, then a tire, now bags?*

Missy tied them to his side and behind him, and anywhere she thought it was needed.

"Buddy, I need you to get used to pulling and hearing weight noises *behind* you. I know you know how to handle a rider and all of that, but I have a new idea for us for future fun." Missy explained as she again picked up the reins and directed Sir Prize back into the meadow. Going left, then right. The plastic bags crinkled all over – behind him, to the side of him – he couldn't get away from it. It was like he was being chased by groceries.

Oh, and don't forget the fun of pulling the tire, Sir Prize thought, unamused by this new activity of Missy's.

Finally, Missy said "whoa" and stopped him. "That's enough for the day, buddy. You did good!" She rewarded Sir Prize with a handful of his favorite apple snacks. She removed all the contraptions, freeing him of the afternoon training.

He wasn't thrilled with this new training, but Missy grinned ear-to-ear. *Next time, I expect a raise in snack payment.*

*****

This new training routine went on for days, perhaps weeks. Sir Prize was not amused by it, but he got used to it. The crinkling bags no longer bothered him. Missy would put on additional tire weight from time to time and he could manage it. On occasion, she would add other noise makers to the end of the straps to change up the training experience. Thankfully she always reinforced it with his favorite apple snacks.

After several weeks of pull training, Sir Prize heard Missy talking with a new voice. The voices grew louder as the humans headed down the steep hill, balancing on the foot path. "Jack, I can't tell you enough how much I appreciate you coming to help. We've been working to get Sir Prize ready for this. I can't wait for our new adventures," Missy said with new-found excitement in her voice.

"Absolutely! Happy to help!" said Jack.

Both now appeared at Sir Prize's stall; he flickered an ear toward her as a hello greeting. Missy handed something to Jack, who then handed out his hand to Sir Prize. *Snacks!* he greedily accepted them, munching loudly. *Ok, we can be friends.*

She brushed off Sir Prize as they continued their chatter. He reached out this nose to smell Jack more, quivering his lips against his jacket seams. *Hey new guy!* Sir Prize welcomed him as he does anyone who greets him with snacks.

Missy grabbed a halter and slipped it over Sir Prize's head. It molded perfectly against the bridge of his nose and over his ears as it always did. They stepped out of the stall and headed behind the barn into the meadow pasture, no different than any other day.

Then he saw it. *A cart!* Sir Prize's eyes widened as memories of Cochise and his owner driving a cart just like that came crashing back into his mind. *Oh, this is bad. Very, very bad.* he grimaced.

Missy walked Sir Prize closer to the cart, letting him see it, sniff it, and get used to its presence. Meanwhile, she and Jack kept talking about it. They were completely oblivious to Sir Prize's distress.

"Ok, when we get ready to hitch him in…" Jack's voice kept a steady pace as Missy went to work. She busied herself with adding straps and buckles to Sir Prize, the same ones that they used during the recent grocery bag and tire trainings.

Are we seriously doing this? Sir Prize hissed at them in this mind.

Missy lifted the cart shafts so they pointed high above Sir Prize's back, rolling the cart forward until the cart was directly behind his tail. She then lowered the shafts on both sides of his body. After a few more adjustments, a few more tugs, he was hitched to the cart!

Oh, I do not like this at all. Sir Prize thought, ears pinned back as far as his forehead muscles would allow. *I am a pony for riders, not…not…playing Rudolf for a day,* he grunted. Sir Prize silently cursed Cochise. *Thanks, neighbor! You gave Missy a new, unnecessary hobby that I must now endure.* He was immediately defiant and rebellious.

Sir Prize instantly flopped down on top of one of the shafts. *Nope.* He didn't care that the cart was still hitched to him. He didn't care that the shaft pushed uncomfortably against his side. *I'm not moving, and you can't make me,* he huffed into the grass tickling his nose.

"Oh, my goodness! I think he just had a heart attack!" exclaimed Jack, running over to check on Sir Prize.

Ha! I got you! Sir Prize smirked, lying very still in opposition.

Missy rolled her eyes. "No. No heart attack. Just one giant toddler tantrum. This is his way of telling us he doesn't like this. Some how, years before I knew him, he learned this little trick. He thinks he'll get out of work by doing this. And I'm worried if we don't get him up, he'll break the shaft he is lying on and the cart will be useless."

Sir Prize watched Missy from the corner of his eye, wondering how she was going to handle this moment. *Will she give in?* As she went to the other side of him, she whispered to him "Oh, I know what you're up to and you don't get a say." She leaned down and pushed on his hips just right so that the pressure forced Sir Prize to adjust. With a little more pressure, she was able to influence him to stand. She immediately rewarded him with treats. "That a boy," she said, nodding in acknowledgement.

"I've never in my life seen a horse do that when hitched to a cart. And I've been doing this for years," Jack said, still astonished by Sir Prize's little act of defiance.

Missy shrugged. "Yeah, when I got him all those years ago, he did that when I tied him into a trailer. At the time, I had the same reaction you did. But now, I know it is his level of defiance. Depending on the situation, he may win." With a smirk she continued, "But not today."

After giving him a couple more treats and more friendly pats, she walked to the cart. She slowly got into it, picked up the reins. She watched Sir Prize's ears, to see if he would pin them back as he did earlier. Nothing. She steadied the reins and commanded "Sir Prize, walk on". This time, Sir Prize moved forward. *Fine.* Sir Prize huffed. "Progress," Missy sighed.

Although Sir Prize was irritated from the cart situation, he always relied on his trust of Missy. In those first few moments of pulling the cart, he analyzed the situation more. *The weight sensation on my chest is the same as before,* he pondered. *The straps are the same, just slightly different experience.* The cart rolled smoothly behind him in the meadow grass. Missy kept encouraging him saying "That a boy, Sir Prize". Chap happily ran by Sir Prize's side. Jack watched in awe with how quickly Sir Prize caught onto the task. In these first few moments of success – for both humans and pony – all seemed well. *I think I deserve more snacks now,* Sir Prize negotiated to himself.

*****

Over the next few months, Missy and Sir Prize sometimes drove through the quiet neighborhood with the cart. People would stop and stare at the unusual sight since Sir Prize was the only pony in this neighborhood. People waved as they drove through the streets. Sometimes children ran along beside them, excitedly laughing.

Sir Prize, Missy, and Chap ready for a cart ride (although Chap seems content to lie in the meadow grass)

One day, Missy and Sir Prize ventured a different route into new neighborhoods, small roads, and finally through a wooded path. They popped out into a clearing and Sir Prize instantly recognized it. This was their previous home, where he and Cecil became best friends, where Cochise demanded respect, and where his last jumped caused his injury.

"Whoa buddy," Missy said as she pulled on the reins cuing him to stop.

Sir Prize halted where the pavement met the grass next to his old pasture. She climbed out of the cart to talk to some old friends, but he paid no attention. He stared at the familiar tree lines, fence rows, and waving grasses. His mind immediately started a movie reel of memories: meeting Cecil, learning to swish his tail more vigorously, seeing his best friend be carried away, the not-so-welcoming Cochise. All the memories were fresh as if they happened yesterday.

Speaking of Cochise, Sir Prize thought. He saw Cochise off in the distance, grazing on the pasture grass as they all used to do in their off-training days.

As Sir Prize stood there, he realized the only thing he missed about this place was Cecil. And Cecil hasn't been around for a while. As soon as Cecil was gone, this place was no longer home.

As if Missy could tell he ended his reminiscing, she climbed back into the cart and took up the reins.

"Ready to go home, Sir Prize?" she asked.

Yes. Yes, I am. Sir Prize raised his head proudly and off they went, back to their meadow. *Let's go home.*

*****

Days and weeks passed with several more cart adventures in the books. By now, Sir Prize was a pro at pulling the cart. The weight of the cart, the feel of the straps, and rein steering was as comfortable to him as his trusty, old halter. When he realized that this contraption no longer bothered him, Honey Girl's voice came back to him: *It's not that bad once you get used to it.* Sir Prize missed his friend so much; but the sadness quickly faded. He truly believed his friend was doing just fine, wherever she was.

As the days grew colder and the day light hours shrunk, Missy didn't use the cart as often. She let Sir Prize take comfort in the coziness of his stall. "It's just not carting weather," she'd say to Sir Prize. She'd layer a blanket onto his back to help with the chill. Although Sir Prize didn't like the cold, he did appreciate the break from working the cart so often.

When the sun warmed winter's wind, Missy prepared the cart for the next season's journeys. She dusted it off, oiled down the leather straps, and checked the cart's wheels for cracks or loose fittings. Their first cart rides would be short, giving Sir Prize the time he needed to reacquaint himself with the workout, building his endurance levels. Within a matter of a few weeks, he would be back to his old self, pulling the cart as if winter never came.

MISSY IS MISSING

Although spring was still weeks away, Missy took advantage of a slightly warmer day to take Sir Prize for a pre-season cart pull. It was short, but the work out expanded his lungs with much-needed fresh air. He felt good after the end of their adventure. *These days are perfect for these work outs!* He was "in the moment" when he noticed a new human walking to the barn. "Carin, meet Sir Prize. Sir Prize, meet Carin," Missy greeted as she unharnessed him from the cart. He wasn't spooked, but always curious. Carin reached out her hand. *Apple snacks!* He eagerly took them as she approached his side.

"Well, aren't you a cutie!" she praised, petting the side of Sir Prize's face. *Why, thank you,* Sir Prized blushed. He looked her over carefully as she continued her conversation with Missy. He tuned out their chatting until he heard the words "farm" and "horses". His ears perked forward to listen more. *Another horse person?* he was intrigued.

"Although I grew up on a farm, but we didn't have horses," Carin paused her story, raising her eyebrows. "We did have a donkey to protect the sheep from other predators. I tried to ride it once, but she wasn't rider broke so that didn't work out as I hoped. We also had cattle, sheep, pigs, and chickens." She continued to scratch on Sir

Prize, with additional nuzzling of her forehead against his. "Taking care of animals is like second nature to me," she said, picking up a pitchfork to help Missy with the stall. She and Missy continued their talk as they worked.

The more friends the merrier, Sir Prize thought. *Usually means more treats for me.*

Missy gave careful instructions on his feeding and exercise routines. "In the morning I give him one flake of hay and one large scoop of feed. While he's eating, I fill his water bucket with fresh water and clean the stall."

Carin asked more questions and by this point Sir Prize wasn't really paying attention; he was too focused on eating his feed. She started to brush his shoulders and back with one of the thick bristle brushes. It made his skin quiver as it tickled his hairs. Sir Prize heard her say "So, Missy, when are you having surgery again? How long will you need help with Sir Prize?"

"I'm having the knee surgery sometime at the end of February or first of March. Because of the steep hill to the house and my therapy, I probably won't get to come see him until sometime in the spring if I'm lucky."

Carin combed his mane near his ears. She leaned in and whispered to Sir Prize "Don't worry, buddy. You'll be in good hands with me! I'll take great care of you while Missy is recovering."

Ok, I don't know what that means, but as long as you feed me snacks, we'll be all good, Sir Prize nuzzled her forehead in return.

For several days both Missy and Carin took care of Sir Prize. Carin became efficient in the feeding routines, but always took extra time to give him treats and loving attention. Sir Prize would gently nudge her with his head; in return, she'd scratch his nose. He felt special now that two people attended to him every day. Then suddenly one day it was just Carin. No Missy.

"Well Sir Prize, it's just you and me now! Missy is recovering from her surgery," she said as she dumped feed into his bucket. Feed dust billowed around its crown.

That evening: "Hi Sir Prize! How about I let you out into the meadow for some free time."

The next day: "Good morning! Do you want to walk around in the meadow while I clean your stall?"

Later that night: "Good evening handsome! How about we go for a walk up the road to get you some exercise!"

Ok, where is Missy? Sir Prize wondered. Although he liked Carin, she was not Missy. *Where could she be? Did she forget about me? What did I do wrong that she doesn't want to be around me anymore?* These were all thoughts swirling in Sir Prize's head as Carin continuously showed up and Missy did not.

Sir Prize noticed that when Carin was around, so was Chap. *Well at least my furry friend is still with me. But he's always with Missy. Why is he around Carin now? Where is Missy?*

Little did Sir Prize know that Carin stopped in at the house to check on Missy and release Chap for some outside fun. Missy continued to heal at the house and was unable to walk down the steep hill to visit her beloved pony.

Most mornings Carin was there just as the sun was rising in the east. Because the meadow was in a valley surrounded by trees, it would be another hour before the sun warmed the shadows. She would whisper "Good morning" quietly to Sir Prize, stirring him from his deepest slumber. As he woke, he often heard an owl hooting deep in the woods. She would open the stall door and lead Sir Prize out to the middle of the meadow. Sometimes deer would stand perfectly still in the creek bed, watching the interruption. These were the most peaceful times in the meadow, just before dawn.

Although Sir Prize was still worried about Missy, he grew to appreciate his new friend. Her routine was a little more relaxed than Missy's. *And no cart adventures!* Sir Prize both loved and hated this realization. No cart meant no Missy. But no cart meant leisurely walks instead. After Carin finished her chores in the stall, she would grab his halter and lead rope off the hooks, shove apple snacks in her pocket, and head over to him to start their daily walks.

She rarely rode on his back. She enjoyed walking at his level, being near his face. This made it more personal for Sir Prize, as if it was two friends out for a stroll. Their walks were silent except for the rhythmic beat of his hooves contacting the pavement. Along both sides of the road were brushes and trees, as if the woods extended their limbs to the road. Since it was still cold and the leaves have not returned, the limbs exposed paths and holes where other animals made a home. One morning, Carin stopped suddenly on the road.

"Wow! Look at that Sir Prize," she whispered. She stared into the weaved and tangled limbs to the right. Sir Prize turned his head, not understanding their broken pace. He noticed that Carin was very still, barely breathing.

In the brush lied a majestic stag deer, with a crown of large, pointed antlers. He camouflaged into the brush background. Carin stayed still. The deer stayed still. Sir Prize stayed still. For a moment, it was if time stopped too. The deer did not seem startled by the sudden visitors; he was confident in his own space, accepting of their pause. After several seconds of appreciating the beautiful creature, Carin slowly turned back to Sir Prize. "Ok boy, let's go. We've disturbed him enough." Not once did the deer move, even as they started their walk again.

Sir Prize realized that Carin's gentle way about her was very similar to

Missy. Whey they weren't walking silently in the mornings, she would open the back doors of the barn and just sit in a chair, watching the meadow wake up – birds chirping and finding food, squirrels jumping between trees, Chap rolling in the grass. She seemed to take solace in the meadow's ambiance. But she wasn't Missy.

Where is Missy? was a constant question in Sir Prize's mind. Although there was no trailer rattling down to the meadow indicating another move, the loss of Missy's daily visits worried him just as much. *I think I would prefer the move at this point. At least I know what comes with that. This not knowing of where she is or if she's ok or when she'll be back bothers me more,* he told himself. *It's like she never said good-bye.* Sir Prize's heart was heavy with dread and missing his human friend.

A STORM OF FEAR, FRENZY, AND FRIENDS

A few weeks after Missy's surgery, spring officially hit the calendar. The season generally brings in rain as the Missouri weather moves from winter cold to summer sun. Since the barn was at the base of a hill, all the rain at the top of the hill ran down to its foundation. If it wasn't raining too hard, this wasn't an issue. But heavy rains made the barn flood in the back storage room. Missy knew this and always kept Sir Prize, his feed, and hay away from that room. Sir Prize doesn't mind a bath but standing water in a stall wasn't good hygiene for any animal, including a pony.

By the time the early flowers bloomed, Missy was finally able to visit Sir Prize on occasion. She used devices called "crunches" … *or were they "crutches"*, Sir Prize corrected himself. *She looks weird. Like now she's a four-legged animal too,* he imagined. He watched her as she awkwardly hobbled around him. She couldn't move around too fast in them. But he didn't care. He was so grateful to see his old friend again. Unfortunately, her visits were still scarce; those days drained her energy and sometimes made her knee sore from the exercise. Between her visits, Sir Prize anxiously awaited to see her again.

One afternoon both Carin and Missy were at the barn for evening feeding time. It mildly rained the last two days, and the sky was still gray, threatening to dump more water onto the meadow. "We'll need to keep an eye on the barn this spring. It has been really wet and sometimes it floods in the barn," Missy warned.

Carin continued with the chores, now a pro at Sir Prize's routine. She went to the storage room and yelled back "yeah, there's definitely some water back here."

"Yeah, that's normal this time of year. But if it goes beyond that room and starts creeping into Sir Prize's stall, we'll have to move him."

Carin looked concerned. "But where would we move him?"

Missy shook her head. "I don't know. But I need to make some calls. I have a bad feeling about this spring."

*****

Hours after Carin and Missy left, the sky was void of light. No stars. No moon. Sir Prize couldn't even see the tree silhouettes. The air was eerily void of wind and noise. He didn't hear any night animals. Even the owls were silent. He twitched his ears and flared his nostrils in anticipation. *Something's happening,* he thought. The short hairs on the back of his shoulders shifted as the scent of the air around him felt charged and wet. Suddenly his stall illuminated from a flash of lightening behind the woods, followed by a crash of thunder. It felt like the meadow was instantly under attack. Sir Prize shuffled back into the stall from fear of what just happened, heart racing from adrenaline. *Oh, my goodness!* he huffed.

Heavy drops of rain hit the roof. One, two, then three or four at a time. It was slow at first. Thunder cracked in the air as water dumped from the sky like someone turned over a bucket from the clouds. Sir Prize heard water slam against the storage windows as the wind whipped it like a rag doll. More lightening filled the sky with day-light radiance. Lightening, then thunder, and rain surrounded the meadow barn for a least a half hour before it settled to a steady rainfall. The thunder and lightning moved on to intimidate others, but the rain continued.

Sir Prize's heart rate started to slow, and he relaxed his ears. For a few more minutes, he listened to the rain hitting the barn roof. He flipped his ears forward to listen for any other sounds of life – or new threats from the sky. Nothing. Just the rain. It was steady, gentle but consistent like a lullaby. The rhythm of the rain lulled him to sleep.

*****

Sir Prize jolted awake. *My hooves are wet!* At first, he thought he was dreaming about being in the creek at the base of the meadow. But it felt too real. His senses snapped to reality. *Oh, my goodness! My stall is flooding! Who can help me? Where's Missy now?* He panicked, eyes wide and shifting, searching in the dark. It was in the middle of the night; no one visits him then. *At this point, where's anyone? Carin? Chap? I need help immediately!*

Sir Prize still couldn't see anything around him but darkness. As he waded around in the water, he felt it rising above his hooves. He anxiously paced the stall, hearing the water slosh against the stall walls. His stall door was locked like always. He had no way to escape.

Sir Prize's thoughts swirled in a storm of concern. He occasionally leaned on the stall door, hoping it would break free. As he leaned harder on the door, he saw a light in the distance. The light danced around in random patterns. His eyes widened as he twitched his ears forward. *What is it now? What could possibly be coming? I wish Missy was here! Or even, Carin! Someone? Anyone!* he shouted in his head. He blew air between his lips, exhaling harshly and making a "flllbbhp" sound.

"Sir Prize!" his heart leaped for joy as he heard Missy's voice! *Oh, how I love this human!* He was instantly relieved she came to help. *She must have sensed something was wrong and came to help me!*

She opened the stall door and turned on the light. She gasped as soon as she saw the water. Still using at least one crutch, she leaned against the door and put a phone by her ear. He heard her talking to various people; then she called Carin.

"Hi Carin! I'm so sorry to call so early in the morning but I'm going to need your help. Sir Prize's stall is flooded, and we need to move him to a nearby facility, an equine therapy service up the road. They have an extra stall they are going to let us use. I don't have a horse trailer to use this quickly, so we'll need to walk him there. I am going to bring my truck down and start gathering some things. Do you think you can come help?" Missy hobbled next to Sir Prize to throw a cover over his back as she listened. "Ok thanks. I'll see you soon. Be sure to wear something that you can get wet. It is still raining."

Move? Sir Prize twitched his ears back. *Did she just say the word 'move' and my name in the same sentence?*

As Missy walked away, Sir Prize's heart rapidly pounded in his chest. He perked his ears as high as they would go. He listened to every noise, sensing every movement. Missy seemed nervous. The last time he sensed this in her was when he injured his leg. He trusted her to be the calm one so that he can be calm. *Something's not right,* he thought.

Soon he heard the truck. He rarely hears the truck at the barn at night. His ears twitched back as it got closer to the barn. Everything seemed off to him. He calculated all the things happening: *water in my stall…Missy at the barn with her truck at night. What could possibly be happening?* he shifted his weight, observing the chaos around him. Missy moved him outside so he didn't stand in the water, but the rain now trickled water down his face.

As he continued to watch Missy's rushed actions, more humans approached the barn. One of them was Sally, Missy's sister. Then he saw a couple of other people he didn't recognize. They packed buckets, feed, hay, brushes, and anything else they could think of into Missy's truck. She directed people where to go since she was unable to lift anything in her one-legged condition. All the people at such an odd time of the night made Sir Prize nervous.

He then noticed Carin walk toward him; he felt a little relief. "Hey boy! You've had quite the night! Well, get ready because we're moving you to a dryer home. You don't want to stay in this wet barn, do you?" she said in a soft and sweet tone. He realized that while Missy was anxious, Carin's demeanor was calm and steady. This soothed his nerves. But he kept an eye on Missy. She seemed overwhelmed.

Carin slid the familiar halter over his ears. She gently said, "Come on, buddy. It's time."

Time for what? What are we doing? Where are we going? It's too dark for a stroll now! Sir Prize hesitated.

Missy now stood at the back of the truck. All the activity stopped, and the group waited for her instructions. The scene reminded Sir Prize of how she took charge during the Animal Planet Day. "Ok. We're ready to go. The new barn is about three miles from here. We'll take the backroads as much as we can so we can avoid heavy traffic. I am going to drive behind all of you with my flashers on so passing drivers can see you. Each of you need to wear your rain gear and keep your flashlights on. I need one person leading the group to warn of obstacles on the road ahead. I need the others on each side of Sir Prize so he doesn't get spooked," Missy was back in that leadership mode Sir Prize remembered so well. Although her voice was calm and clear, there was a still a hint of uncertainty.

Wait. Sir Prize realized. *And did I just hear her say 'new barn'? What?*

As the group walked along the road, Missy's truck's headlights illuminated the path ahead. Unfortunately, the group had to walk on the side of the road where there was mud and sometimes uneven ground. They walked slowly, stopping at times while Sir Prize's helpers checked the ground in front of them. The headlights made new, long shadows from the group and objects around them. These shadows confused him. If he just relied on his sight, he would have panicked just like those other horses did that day on the trail. He remembered on that day he listened to Missy's voice. But he didn't hear her voice this time. *Where is Missy now?* The only voice he recognized was Carin's.

"If we see cars coming toward us, be sure to move your flashlights back and forth to warn the drivers to slow down," she said to the others.

"Let's keep a good pace so we can get there sooner rather than later," she eventually said.

Her voice was calm. And soon they giggled and chatted about various stories Sir Prize didn't understand. *Even though it is dark…even though it is raining, these humans are still having fun!* He then realized the entire group was there to take care of him. *Just like I took care of that little girl that one day.* He started to feel ok again. He started to think maybe the new home will be just as fun as his meadow. *After all, I was able to be happy there. Surely, I can be happy at the new place. Right?*

A BARN OF HOPE

"Hey Sir Prize, we're here!" said Carin. It was hard to see in the dark but thankfully the rain slowed down to a peaceful drizzle. The thunder and lightning were now a distant memory.

Sir Prize saw some lights around a large building. *Is this the new barn?* Sir Prize took in the size of the structure. *It seems too large for a small pony like me.* And just as the thought finished, Sir Prize recognized at that this point, he didn't care where they were. He was tired and desired overdue rest.

He finally saw Missy hop out of the truck that followed the group. She hobbled over to someone in a coat near the barn. After a few nods of the heads and a quick handshake, the stranger opened the barn door. Carin carefully led Sir Prize through the barn. From the barn entrance, Sir Prize saw a massive area supported by old beams and a wash area for horses. To the left were several stalls. The sleepy horses grunted at the rude awakening of lights, indicating this was not their normal wake-up time. All but one stall had horses in them. *Horses! Not ponies! Full, grown, much-taller-than-me horses!* Sir Prize observed.

Each horse walked to their stall window to see what was happening. They did not look happy. Sir Prize understood how they felt; he didn't like being awakened in the middle of the night either. *Sorry for disturbing your beauty rest.* Sir Prize sheepishly looked at them as he passed. A few of them snorted at his presence.

"You'll have that far stall at the end," directed the stranger. Sir Prize sarcastically shouted in his mind *Really? You're going to parade me past each of these horses? Haven't we bothered them enough?* He prayed for the ability to speak human to explain to them that this didn't win him any popularity points with his new neighbors.

The Longview Farm Park barn in Town & Country, MO. Sir Prize temporarily stayed here when his barn flooded in 2004 (picture taken 2021)

Once in his stall, Carin took the rain sheet off Sir Prize. It was drenched from the rain and drizzle, but it kept him dry during their walk. She brushed him down, complimenting his accomplishment. "Sir Prize you did great! I know this sucks, but you're safe and that's what's most important." She patted his face, kissed his nose, and fed him some apple treats. *She knows me so well!* Sir Prize silently thanked her.

As Carin and the others tried to make his stall feel at home, he took in his new surroundings. The smell of the barn was just like the Mason barn with the scents of other horses. His stall had tall walls so he couldn't see who was next to him, but he could hear a horse next door. The only door to the stall also led to what appeared to be a path to a larger field. It was hard to see in the dark, but Sir Prize could see a sliver of morning light on the horizon.

The small stall wasn't too much different than home. But the old, familiar feelings of being homesick crept in again. He felt out of place, nervous about the other horses that he could hear and smell. It was now close to sunrise, and he was depleted. The adrenaline of the night's storm, walk, and new place were wearing off and he just wanted to sleep.

"I hate this," Missy whispered to Carin. She stared at Sir Prize as she added hay to his stall. "We are fortunate that the city is letting us use this space but animals not familiar with each other are unpredictable. Sir Prize hasn't lived around other horses in a while and sometimes horses can be territorial. I have to talk to the barn manager on how we can give him pasture time so he isn't stuck in this stall all day every day."

"Well, he should rest for now, probably. Let's come back in a few hours once it is daylight and figure it out then," said Carin. Missy agreed.

Both patted Sir Prize on the neck, said their goodbyes, and left the stall. Everyone left. Soon all he could hear were a few horses huffing and pawing. Even though he didn't like where he was and his mind raced about all the excitement that just happened, his body was so tired. Without trying, Sir Prize drifted to sleep.

*****

After a few hours of sleep, he heard voices in the distance and a large barn door opening. He didn't recognize these voices. One of them came closer to his stall. "We got a new roommate for our horses," someone said. The voices got louder; unexpectedly a visitor stood in front of Sir Prize's stall. "Well, hi there!" she said. She reached out to pet him. He was a little apprehensive but usually people are nice to him. He slowly walked up to smell her hand. She moved one of her fingers to tickle his nose. Sir Prize stepped back and walked to the hay to have some breakfast; he ignored her begging to come back.

"Well, I guess he'll make friends over time. Do we know how long he's staying?" she asked someone else. Sir Prize heard someone answer but didn't understand what they said. His visitor turned and walked to the wall of the barn near his stall. She unlocked it and opened it. Sir Prize's eyes widened when he realized this extra-large door was right next to his stall. As his eyes adjusted to the sudden sunshine, he could see a large parking area, more people, and some trees off in the near distance. *Maybe they have a meadow like my barn! Maybe this place will be ok after all!* Sir Prize hoped.

Sir Prize heard noises at his stall door behind him. When he turned, he witnessed a couple of the horses sticking their heads right into his stall, invading his assigned space. The door lock creaked in resistance to their weight. They couldn't get into his stall, but they made their presence known to Sir Prize. Since he was the new addition to the barn, he had everyone's interest that day.

Well, what do we have here? One of the larger horses sniffed the air in Sir Prize's stall.

Looks like a small horse. Why is he so small? Another horse slipped his head into the stall, pushing the first horse out of the way.

Oh, he's definitely not one of us. The comments kept rolling.

Sir Prize finally turned his back on them and stayed in the furthest corner of his stall so they couldn't touch him. He was not in a good mood considering the night he had. And he certainly was not in a mood to make new friends. *And from the comments, they don't want to be friends neither,* he concluded.

Oh look, he's scared! They all pushed together, thudding against the door. They made final comments just before each horse swaggered down a fenced path. *Why do some horses have to be such jerks?* Sir Prize fumed.

One horse stayed behind and peeked through the door like the others did. *Don't mind them. They don't like change. It's their shame they can't see the beauty you bring.* Sir Prize didn't respond. He didn't know what to say. The nicer horse slowly walked away, looking back at Sir Prize one last time before disappearing down the same fenced path.

Although Sir Prize appreciated the last horse's efforts to cheer him up, every nerve and every negative emotion hummed inside his head. He instantly didn't have an appetite. He stayed in the same corner most of the morning, pouting about this new sudden change in his life. He kept thinking to himself *I want my meadow back. I want my barn back. I want Missy, Chap, and Carin back. I just want to go back!*

He began to pace his stall with frustration and anxiety. He reminisced about all the other times he was around horses or moved. He had never felt ashamed of being a pony before, of being small. He realized that all the horses he'd been around were of various sizes. *"Why does my size matter now?*

He stopped pacing as he heard more human voices. He perked his ears forward, hoping for a familiar voice. As he stood in his stall listening to humans talk, he finally heard them. *Missy and Carin! Oh, thank God! Perhaps now we can go home!*

"Unfortunately, the barn will need major repairs that I just can't do right now since I'm still healing. Terry will help me, thankfully," Sir Prize heard Missy say. "And I can't miss work much more since I had to take off for my surgery."

"I understand. We'll have to make this his new home for now. What did the barn manager say?" Carin asked as she took his water bucket to fill it.

"Well, Sir Prize is welcome for now but I suspect they will need us to move soon," Missy said as she filled his bucket with feed. "This place actually does therapeutic riding for children. Perhaps we can use Sir Prize for some of the smaller kids as a 'thank you' for letting him stay."

"That sounds fun!" Carin said, smiling as she fed Sir Prize an apple snack. She walked to the back of the stall. "What about letting him have some pasture time? What did they say?"

"We still have to work that out. The horses have priority but perhaps we can walk him around the pasture with a halter if they are ok with that," said Missy. She sounded tired.

Unexpectedly, Sir Prize heard another voice. This is the same voice from last night who helped open the barn to them. "Ah, there's the manager now," said Missy.

"Good morning!" said the manager. "Looks like you all were able to make yourselves at home here. What's his name again?"

"Sir Prize," said Missy.

"Sir Prize! What a great name!" said the manager.

Missy continued. "Is there any way we can get him some pasture time during the day? I don't want to take away from your schedule but even if it is 30 minutes or an hour, that would be great!"

The manager scrunched her brows together. "We could probably work it in, but it would have to be early in the morning or late in the day because the other horses have priority due to their schedule."

Missy added, "Ok that sounds great. We'll take whatever you're willing to do. We just appreciate you letting us stay here while we fix our barn. Also, if there is anything we can do to help around here, please let us know. We want to give back as a thank you for letting him stay. What do you say to letting Sir Prize be one of your helpers with the therapy classes? He's very calm around the kids."

The manager smiled and said "Sure! We'd love the help. We won't be able to use him for the program because of our rules, but you're welcome to volunteer and walk along the horses if you'd like. Let's see what we can do."

And just like that, Carin and Missy became assistants for the program! Missy looked at Sir Prize and said "Well, you may not be able to have kids on your back, but we can get you out and walk you around from time to time."

Sir Prize didn't understand. For the first time, he wanted to have a halter on his face and a lead rope in Missy's hand. *Home. Now.* He commanded.

THE LEGEND OF THE STORM PONY

To Sir Prize's disappointment, they did not go home. As the days passed, Sir Prize slowly got used to his new surroundings and the new daily schedule. Carin still took care of him in the mornings and nights, but Missy was able to visit more often. Missy introduced him to the barn volunteers, to the park patrons, and barn visitors. The kids loved him!

"So, this is a pony? Not a horse?" asked one small child.

"Yes! As a matter of fact, do you know how brave he is?" Missy asked. The kid shook his head, eagerly waiting to hear the story. "Do you remember that big storm we had a month ago? Remember all the thunder and lightning?" The child nodded with excitement. She continued to tell the story of how they walked there in the night, through the rain, and made this a new home. As she told the story, other parents and children surrounded her, intently listening.

Soon, people titled Sir Prize the "storm pony". The barn volunteers often stopped by his stall, fed him treats, and gave loving pats on his nose. Missy repeated her story often, bragging of Sir Prize's bravery. Sometimes people would ask, "Is the storm pony still here?" Sir Prize could not understand why he was so famous!

On occasion, Missy or Carin walked Sir Prize around the park grounds. He learned that he now lived at a place called Longview. But the lessons they did at this barn were different than other horse communities he experienced. He observed the volunteers work with people of various ages and sizes, but mostly children. Each child was carefully placed onto a horse by the volunteers. Two volunteers slowly strolled with each horse and rider. As he watched, memories of his training days flashed into his mind. He realized that he missed working with children.

One day, Missy led Sir Prize closer to the pasture fence, near what appeared to be a platform or dock. This allowed him a closer watch on how they managed the rides. He studied interactions between the volunteers and the riders. He watched as a parent pushed a wheelchair up the platform. *Is that child in his own cart?* Sir Prize wondered. The volunteers lifted the child out of the wheelchair and onto the waiting horse. Sir Prize widened his eyes with wonderment. *I…I don't think I've ever seen this before,* he thought. He continued to watch the two volunteers with the rider. Instead of "move your weight forward" or "pull back on the reins" they gave commands like "reach high to the sky" or "move your arms out as far as you can". Sir Prize found this odd. *Why are they doing that? That's not how you ride a horse!* He kept watching out of curiosity, not sure how a child can learn to ride like that.

When the volunteers finished the lesson, Sir Prize watched as they stopped the tall horse at the platform. They lifted the child out of the saddle and placed him back into his wheelchair. Sir Prize noticed that the child's legs could not move and that the volunteer had to move them for him. Sir Prize twitched his ears forward and raised his head to get a better view. *Oh my! This is a special place indeed!* His heart swelled with awareness and empathy. He realized this was no ordinary training barn. *These people are here because the horses help these children. The children are so happy to be riding a horse that they don't realize they are exercising too!*

Sir Prize was amazed at this insight. However, the intense studying of the riding lessons made him hungry. He leaned his head down for a bite of juicy grass stalks.

"Sir Prize, the storm pony!" the child in the wheelchair called out.

"That pony is so fun!" said a volunteer, waving from the platform. "The kids just love seeing him here."

*****

Whether Sir Prize was in his stable, in the pasture, or taking a stroll with Missy or Carin, the volunteers and children made extra time to say hello. The children would stop by before or after their therapy session, insisting on seeing "the storm pony". Seeing children again lifted his spirits. They were all so friendly and made him feel welcomed.

But he still wasn't welcomed by most of the horses. Some of the horses bullied him by biting him, kicking him, or chasing him in the pasture. Like many other animal packs or herds, there is a "pecking order" or dominance hierarchy within the equine life. And the horses at this barn made it known that he was at the bottom of the acceptance list. This physical and psychological challenge was new to Sir Prize. He didn't have the demeanor or the stature to protect himself against the bullying horses. He was grateful when the nicer horse was with him; together they stayed away from the others. The barn staff quickly recognized that Sir Prize's pasture time had to be managed different for his own safety.

Although, the pasture time adjustment helped Sir Prize's anxiety of his current living space, he still felt very home sick. *Am I ever going back to my meadow?*

As the weeks passed, the weather continued to warm and rain became less frequent. The barn volunteers would arrive early for feeding of the other horses but opened the barn door next to his stall. The early morning sun would shine into Sir Prize's space, tiny dust particles sparkled in the rays. He knew that Missy or Carin would soon arrive. Every morning he hoped it would be the day to go home; so far, that wish was denied.

One morning, Missy arrived at the barn, her hair shimmered in the sun's rays. The weather was perfect outside. Sir Prize was ready to be out in the pasture, but he longed to be home in his own meadow. If Missy or Carin was around, their presence suppressed his home sick feeling.

"Look at you! Don't you seem happy today?" she said as she entered his stall. She patted his neck and nuzzled against his nose. For a moment, Sir Prize was at peace.

She wiped dirt off his back with her leathered, calloused hands. She grabbed his brush and swept his hairs into place. As soon as she started to comb out his mane and tail, his ears stood at attention. She doesn't usually do that unless there was something big happening and she wanted to show him off.

As she took care of his stall and his looks, he noticed a lot of activity happening outside the barn door. *Is it a party?* he thought.

After Missy slid the halter over his ears and tucked it under his chin, he observed she wasn't using her crutch anymore. There was a limp, but she no longer needed aid. *She must be healed! Does this mean I get to go home soon?*

Sir Prize was overjoyed with this assumption and for a few moments, daydreamed about the return home to his meadow. But that fantasy was cut short as soon as he saw the cart. *Wait – the cart? She brought the cart? Why is the cart here?* He stood astonished. *This can't be…* he looked around and another observation hit him: people were waiting.

A few of the barn volunteers from that first stormy night gathered around the cart. "This is so neat!" said one of them. Sir Prize couldn't get a good view of who made the comment, but he appreciated the attention.

"I figured giving free rides in the cart is our way of saying thank you to the organization for hosting us while we fixed the barn back home," Missy explained.

"This is great! The kids will love this! He has become quite the celebrity since he came here. We just love having him here," said another volunteer. "In case you haven't noticed, we get more visitors now that he's around," she chuckled.

"I don't think I realized that!" said Missy. "But he loves everyone, including children."

More people came over to see this unusual pony and cart combination. Missy welcomed anyone who came over for questions. *Always the trainer,* Sir Prize amused.

"Can we ride with you?" one child asked

"Absolutely! That is why we are here! Make sure your parents are ok with it though," Missy instructed, nodding to the parents who stood near-by.

Soon, Sir Prize felt Missy take on the reins and command "walk on" just like they always did back at the meadow. She guided him to the edge of the park and made a return trip. At the end of the first trip, he noticed more people lined up, all waiting for a ride on his cart. His heart swelled with pride and appreciation at the love this small community showed him.

These people really love me. They really love me! Sir Prize realized. *All these strangers, all these people that have known me for such a short time, they really love me.*

Each ride, each turn, each giggle, Sir Prize pulled with more pride. It was one of the happiest days that he can remember in a very long time – *well, since I arrived here*, he thought. Oh sure, he missed his home. But right now, in this moment, with these people smiling over him, pulling this cart on this day, he was on cloud nine.

Saint Louis Post Dispatch newspaper article featuring Sir Prize and Missy (2004). At the time, there was controversy on Sir Prize's stay at the Longview Farm Park barn since he was not officially a part of the equine therapy program that resided in the barn.

On his last turn, he spotted a little more commotion with people dressed in odd outfits. *I've never seen someone dressed up so much* he thought. They pointed in his direction; he was still several yards away but understood he was the topic of conversation.

As Missy slowed Sir Prize to a stop, the dressed-up gentleman approached them.

"Hi Missy! I'm the mayor. We chatted on the phone about Sir Prize a while back." He paused to look over Sir Prize and the cart. "This is incredible! Do you mind if the reporter and I talk to you for a few minutes?" Missy nodded and gracefully climbed down from the cart.

Reporter? Mayor? What does that mean? Sir Prize thought. His thoughts were interrupted with another person circling in front of Sir Prize, holding a device to their face. All he could hear was clicking, then buzzing, clicking, then buzzing.

"Say 'cheese'," the person said, holding the camera right in front of Sir Prize. The camera clicked then buzzed again as the person's fingers fiddled with controls on the device. As much as he loves attention, sometimes having new people around all the time can be exhausting.

The afternoon ride activities wound down to a hush. Missy continued her conversations with the mayor but started to unhitch Sir Prize. The children that rode with Sir Prize tagged behind their parents, climbing into their vehicles for a more modern ride. The sun hung in the sky, indicating that the evening feed activities were near. The enthusiasm that once filled the air slowly faded into the wind. Sir Prize's soul wrestled to hang onto the amazing feeling he felt all afternoon. *I don't want this to end* he bummed.

For so many months, he was alone in his meadow. Today he realized how much he missed barn activities like this. In his younger, non-injured days he was ready for the training, for the trails, for the social life between humans and horses. After the passing of his friend, his soul felt – *empty*, he finished his thought. Then came the injury and his body felt – *broken*, he concluded. But today – today he was healthy and happy. His soul and body felt – *as one*, he noted. Today, he was the Sir Prize that earned his title so long ago. And although he felt so proud of himself for today, his body reminded him that he was no longer that younger pony with fresh ambitions. He surrendered to his reality of an early turn-in.

Missy, the mayor, and the reporter continued the conversation at his stall. Chap sat in the corner, away from the commotion. He seemed tired too. They looked at each other with an understanding of *yep – busy day*. Sir Prize dunked his head into his feed bucket, famished from pulling the cart. He mostly tuned out the human discussion, but one thing made his tired ears perk with excitement.

"…we are so grateful for you allowing us to stay here," Missy again stated. "Soon we'll be heading home. Repairs are almost done."

"Well, I know there has been some controversy of him being here considering he wasn't officially a part of the therapy program; however, we're a community and we need to help each other when we can. Plus," the mayor pointed to Sir Prize, "he is loved by all."

Wait, I'm going home? Did I just hear that? Sir Prize focused on what Missy said. Suddenly, his soul was rejuvenated for the second time that day. But his heart's pace quickened with the anxiety of – *but when?*

*****

Later the next week, Sir Prize enjoyed some much-needed pasture time when he saw Missy's truck parked near the barn entrance. The sun warmed his back as he returned to his feast. He snorted the grass away from his nostrils for a deeper bite. Suddenly, he heard what sounded like buckets banging. He looked up, chewing his latest bite. Missy put the bucket into the back of her truck bed. *That usually means one thing!* His curiosity got to him as he started to walk to the white fence leading to the barn.

Sir Prize reached the barn just as Missy finished packing his stall items into her truck. She turned around and faced Sir Prize, halter in hand.

"Hey beautiful," she called to him. She put the halter on and patted my neck. "You ready to go home?" His ears perked. *Is this happening? Don't play me!*

Missy instructed a couple of friends to help with a few other items. But Sir Prize didn't pay any attention; he was too excited. *I am going home!*

"We'll have to walk him back," Missy sighed. "I still do not have a horse trailer." But he was ready. It's a lovely day. No storms.

As they prepared to leave, the barn volunteers came over to say good-bye. Some of them brought Sir Prize treats which, of course, he accepted with glee. "Bye Sir Prize," said one volunteer, as she wrapped her arms around his neck. "You will be so missed."

Missy reached out her hand to the barn manager, shaking it with a firm grip. "Thank you so very much for letting him stay as we repaired his barn. I'm sorry it took longer than we liked but knowing he was welcomed here made me feel so much better," she said. She sounded funny and there were tears in her eyes. The last time Sir Prize saw tears like that was when she had to move him there. *Humans are funny with their crying. Today's a good day. Why the water works?*

"We will miss Sir Prize. He was a pleasant addition, and a surprise for the kids. No pun intended," said the barn manager with a playful wink in his direction. "The kids will miss him, but they will understand that he will be home."

They strolled down the parking lot, out onto the road. It was in the middle of the day, so the traffic was minimal. As they rounded the corner of the park, Sir Prize took one last look at the white fence, pasture, and barn that he called home for a few months. *Although I'll miss the beauty of this place, I know that my happy place resides in the meadow.* And without a second glance, Sir Prize focused on the road ahead. *And there isn't a cloud in sight.*

LONGVIEW FARM PARK & EQUINE THERAPY ASSISTANCE

In the story, Sir Prized temporarily moved to a barn at Longview Farm Park (Town and Country, MO) which hosted an equine therapy program. Since Sir Prize's stay in 2004, the facilities have been updated and the equine therapy organizations have changed; however, the importance of equine therapy services remain the same and continue to grow. They provide joy to children and adults while developing or strengthening their mental and physical capabilities. If you volunteer at an equine therapy program, you may make friends with a special four-legged animal while making a difference in someone's life.

The pictures in this chapter are from the fall of 2020 and February 2021.

The barn in Longview Farm Park was built in 1893 but underwent necessary updates overtime to maintain the support and appeal.

Beautiful hand-painted mural at the walkway to the stables.

The stable and wash areas for the horses.

The stall where Sir Prize stayed during his time at the facility. This stall was at the far end of the barn.

Therapy-assisting horses, Buddy and Sarge (2021).

Picture of the ramp that is used to help riders get onto the horses. The horses will stand to the side near an opening and volunteer assistants will help the rider safely and securely get onto the horse. The assistants will then guide the horses around the pasture.

UPDATES ON MISSY & SIR PRIZE

 Sir Prize passed away in November of 2005. His strength and mobility deteriorated due to a degenerative condition in his tendons, most likely due to repeated jumping events in his early days (according to his vet). In memory, Missy has Sir Prize's bridle hung in her office along with a painting of Sir Prize that a student gave her.

Missy now lives in Oregon with her husband, working and training horses at their boarding barn.

Missy and Carin both want people to remember Sir Prize for what he was – a gentle, loving soul to all. He was happiest around his human friends: trail riding, eating snacks, or just being with them at the barn or in the pasture.

ABOUT THE AUTHOR

Carin Thamke grew up on a farm in rural, southeast Missouri which ignited the love of agriculture in her soul. She studied Agricultural Journalism at the University of Missouri-Columbia and moved to the Saint Louis, Missouri area after graduating. She currently works within the agriculture industry in business and IT strategy.

She's married with three children, including two stepchildren. When she's not working, she loves to ride her motorcycle, watch her daughter's musical performances, and relax at their family cabin. She and her husband plan to move to southeast Missouri after they retire.

I enjoyed writing this book and sharing Sir Prize's story. I think there are many aspects of these events that teach us all lessons about animal behaviors, building trust with your animals, and helping others in time of need. Thanks to all of you who have supported me during this writing journey. Thank you in advance to all of my readers. This is for you. - Carin

Made in the USA
Columbia, SC
13 January 2023

75013181R10068